COUNTRY ESCAPES

CONTRIBUTING EDITORS **BO NILES** AND **KATHERINE SORRELL**

COUNTRY ESCAPES

INSPIRATIONAL HOMES IN THE HEART OF THE COUNTRY

RYLAND

PETERS

& SMALL

LONDON NEW YORK

SENIOR DESIGNER Sally Powell

SENIOR EDITOR Henrietta Heald

PICTURE AND LOCATION RESEARCH

Emily Westlake

PRODUCTION Paul Harding

ART DIRECTOR Gabriella Le Grazie

PUBLISHING DIRECTOR Alison Starling

First published in the United Kingdom in 2004 by
Ryland Peters & Small
Kirkman House
12–14 Whitfield Street
London W1T 2RP
www.rylandpeters.com

10 9 8 7 6 5 4 3 2 1

Text copyright © Ros Byam Shaw, Jo Denbury,
Leslie Geddes-Brown, Vinny Lee, Judith Miller,
Ryland Peters & Small 2004
Design and photographs copyright
© Ryland Peters & Small 2004

ISBN 1 84172 678 8

A CIP record for this book is available from the British
Library.

Printed and bound in China.

contents

introduction

by Bo Niles

Not so very long ago, when much of the Western world was primarily an agrarian society, living in the country meant living off the land. Go back two or three generations and most people will recall someone who tilled the soil. Time, though, has romanticized our view of how our ancestors lived. Many of us nurture a nostalgic vision of rural life in past ages as 'simple'. Country living was never simple. Not at all. Even so, the simple life is what many people drawn to making a full-time or weekend home in the country hope to enjoy.

Elemental to that vision is a yearning for a connection with nature. Even when nature is tamed to nothing more than a swathe of lawn flanked by hedges or flower beds, the essentials – trees, sky, sun, fresh air and water – offer succour and solace from the hectic bustle of the everyday. Houses in rural settings 'converse' with the land that surrounds them. The conversation may be serious or it may be joyful. It may be playful, conveying a sense of the picturesque, or it may be contemplative and serenely sensitive to the vagaries of nature – and to the fragile ecologies that bind us all.

One dialogue that often takes place in a country house involves how to bring the outdoors inside. Homes engaged in this form of communication open themselves up via expanses of glass or French windows, or screened or open porches or verandas, which blur the separation between interior rooms

and what's outside. Some homes, too, allude to the external through an inspired use of natural materials such as wood and stone and even, occasionally, water.

Another dialogue is with the contents of the house. First and foremost, furnishings must be comfortable and inviting. In many country homes, furnishings also reflect personal connections with – and affection for – antiques, and include collections that coalesce harmoniously and speak to their owners' generous notions of well-being.

All the country escapes that appear in this book convey a relaxed decorating style that not only celebrates rural roots but also expresses a warm, welcoming, wholesome lifestyle that preserves the traditions and ideals of family. These houses, be they rugged or romantic, reaffirm the values of what we perceive in our hearts to be at the heart of country life: authenticity, honesty, resilience, fortitude and intimacy.

Finally, the houses featured here celebrate their links with those earlier generations who lived on the land. In doing so, they bequeath a lasting legacy to their owners – to be loving stewards of their homes and of the countryside that embraces them. This is crucial, for the truth about what rural life is and means today lies within us: in how we hope to live as nurturing, environmentally friendly human beings, shed of pretence and pretension. In sum, this is what country living – and the simple life – is all about, redefined for the modern world.

traditional

Traditional homes proudly proclaim their ancestry by subscribing to the architectural vernacular that is their heritage. Dwelling places as diverse as a log cabin in Kentucky, a parsonage in Connecticut, a *mas* near the French Riviera, a manor house on the île de Ré off the coast of Brittany and a cottage in the Welsh borders are each rooted in a particular time and locality. The owners of traditional country houses such as these honour their provenance, undertaking only gentle restoration and adaptation so that they can retain the soul and spirit of place. In some houses, that air of authenticity is reinforced through a love of period furnishings and accessories – or reproductions that are exact copies. In others, such as a lavishly decorated house in East Anglia, a more flowery formality prevails. Such is the harmony of a traditional outlook that gentility always reigns.

museum piece

One of the reasons why country living is so popular is that it takes us back to our roots and, in the process, allows us to experience the so-called 'simple life'. Americans pay homage to their rural heritage at living-history museums such as Conner Prairie, located in the heart of the American Midwest. These re-creations offer an opportunity to observe the customs of the country at a particular period. In doing so, they also enrich the lives of modern visitors.

ABOVE **The back entry into the museum's Golden Eagle Inn leads into the kitchen; hooks on the wall-hung yoke were used to carry buckets.**

FAR LEFT **The Whitaker Store shows the self-effacing style of architecture that predominated in the East and Midwest in the mid-19th century. Columns are boxed; shutter planks are joined with boards. The bench is a simple half-log on legs.**

LEFT **The kitchen of the Curtis House is equally unpretentious. Rough-hewn boards and beams are whitewashed to amplify light; floors are left unpolished. Windows and door are finished off with half-round moulding and painted red.**

The idea of the open-air museum originated with Skansen, an assembly of rural buildings transported to the outskirts of Stockholm. Other countries emulated the Swedish prototype, but none more enthusiastically than the USA, which now has more than 150 living-history museums, all aiming to educate and engage the public with tours, meals and demonstrations of time-honoured crafts – some during overnight and weekend stays.

Conner Prairie in Fishers, Indiana, which has over 320,000 visitors each year, reflects life on the Great Plains at three points in Indiana's history: 1816, 1836 and 1886. Named after William Conner, a fur trader, land speculator, Indian agent and Indiana state representative, the museum is made up of more than 45 buildings in a space of some 560 hectares (1,400 acres). Since Conner married a Native

HOMESTEADS SUCH AS THE CURTIS HOUSE, WHICH ONCE BELONGED TO A BLACKSMITH, THE CAMPBELL HOUSE, HOME OF THE RESIDENT DOCTOR, AND THE WHITAKER GENERAL STORE PROVIDE VISUAL INSIGHTS INTO A FASCINATING PERIOD OF AMERICAN HISTORY.

LEFT **The Whitaker Store sold slates and schoolbooks as well as journals and special Bibles known as 'hieroglyphic Bibles', which were used as teaching aids. Shaker seeds were boxed and sold by a branch of Shakers who lived in Pleasant Hill, Kentucky.**

ABOVE LEFT **The resident physician was a Dr Campbell, a landowner who accumulated his wealth through land sales. His pantry exhibits a fine collection of baskets.**

ABOVE RIGHT **A dresser in Dr Campbell's house displays a collection of 'Blue Italian' transferware manufactured by Spode and imported from England. The spoons, all pewter, were crafted locally.**

OPPOSITE **One wall in the Whitaker Store comprises a huge, hand-built cupboard for storing stoneware made by modern potters affiliated with Conner Prairie. Drawers once held nails, flints for rifles and seeds, among other things.**

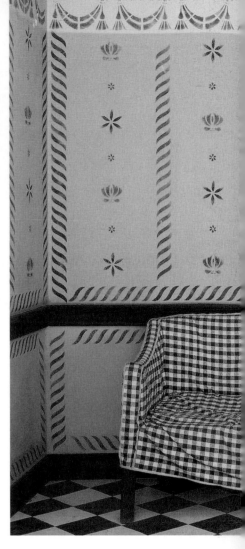

LEFT, ABOVE AND OPPOSITE, ABOVE The parlour walls in the Curtis House were stencilled with coordinating motifs in the Federal style. Blacksmith Curtis brought the parlour settee with him from New York; all other furnishings were purchased locally. Like the painted chequerboard floor, the stencils were restored by Connor Prairie experts to show the patina of age.

OPPOSITE, BELOW Conner Prairie's resident carpenter, a Mr McClure, made a rope-bed with remarkable turnings. The wool and cotton cover has a reproduction 1830s pattern.

HALLMARKS OF THE FEDERAL STYLE INCLUDE THE AMERICAN EAGLE FLYING ABOVE THE CENTRE OF THE MANTELPIECE AND THE SWAG THAT SWOOPS AROUND THE PERIMETER OF THE ROOM BELOW THE CEILING.

American woman of the local Lenape tribe, one area is devoted to an Indian camp and a trading post that was established here before Indiana achieved statehood. Another is dedicated to a village that represents pioneer life on the prairie; yet another to a working farm. Conner's own Federal-style brick home remains on its original site.

Interpreters wearing period costume involve visitors in such a way that they can participate in hands-on activities characteristic of the mid-19th century. Some interpreters lead classes in crafts such as tin-smithing and forging iron; others demonstrate timber-framing techniques, how to make a stepstool, and how to weave cloth on a hand loom.

Visitors who stay overnight or for weekends at the six-bedroom Zimmerman Farm perform tasks such as chopping firewood, peeling vegetables and milking cows, and assist in seasonal activities such as making maple sugar, shearing sheep or bringing in the harvest.

For most visitors, though, touring the various buildings on the property is what teaches them the most about the past. Homesteads such as the Curtis House, which belonged to a blacksmith, and the Whitaker Store, a mercantile operation, offer visual evidence of a fascinating period in American history.

stage struck

As pioneers in a still-youthful and untamed America pressed westwards during the 18th and 19th centuries, they created a network of roads called turnpikes, which were punctuated with roadside inns, taverns and stage stops where weary travellers by wagon train and stage coach could rest themselves and their horses before setting off on the next leg of their journey.

LEFT **Like many of its kind, this stage stop in Kentucky was built of logs. Expanded in the early 20th century, the building and its new wing were both sheathed in clapboard. The current owners removed the boards on the original section, re-exposing the oak logs.**

ABOVE **One of the house's two front doors leads directly into the family room; the other, matching door leads into the living room. Both are painted a weathered slate blue.**

One heavily used route took wagon trains through northern Kentucky to the Ohio River, but the advent of the railway in the mid-19th century made it virtually obsolete; turnpikes reverted to quiet byways and stage stops all but disappeared – or were converted into houses for the industrious immigrant farmers who arrived in droves to settle and develop the fertile farmland.

The scenario was familiar to the current owners of one roadside stopping place that the wife's grandparents had bought in the early 20th century when they were expanding their tobacco farm. Like many structures on the 200 hectare (500 acre) estate, it was used as an outbuilding. By the time the granddaughter inherited the house a decade ago, it had doubled in size, but it had also deteriorated badly. The new

owners considered razing the building, but a knowledgeable friend convinced them of its historical importance. Once the decision to rehabilitate the house had been made, a local firm that restores log cabins entered the fray. The couple also brought in Beverly Jacomini, a friend and interior designer whose work often involves infusing new life into old structures. This was, after all, to be a holiday retreat and part-time retirement home, and the couple wanted it to be easy to maintain, so they wouldn't worry about it between visits.

One reason why the granddaughter loved the house was that it was among the smallest on the farm. Its very petiteness, though, posed a challenge. When the house was expanded,

WHEN THIS AREA OF KENTUCKY WAS SPARSELY SETTLED, AND NATIVE AMERICANS STILL THREATENED THE PIONEERS, MANY FRONTIER FAMILIES PUT A SO-CALLED 'INDIAN BAR', HELD BY A PAIR OF IRON BRACKETS, ACROSS THEIR DOORS AS A SECURITY MEASURE.

ABOVE The Jenny Lind-style spool bed is a cherished piece that belonged to the owner's grandmother, who lived in a bigger house on the farm. Some of the logs here and elsewhere in the cabin have been salvaged from other outbuildings to replace those that had gone rotten.

RIGHT The dining area, which includes a galley kitchen, occupies a wing at the back of the house, behind the living room. Mismatched chairs flank the table. The piesafe, or storage cabinet, stands in for kitchen cupboards; it is an original Kentucky piece that returned to its home state after a spell in Houston.

ABOVE An antique church pew, made locally, stands against a pumpkin-painted wall in the living room, which also serves as the front hall. Jacomini chose this burnished colour because the porches reduced the amount of light that could penetrate into the space. Stairs ascend to the master bedroom.

RIGHT A separate set of stairs in the family room lead to the guest bedroom. The brackets – designed to hold an 'Indian bar' to protect against Native Americans – and the door pull are wrought-iron reproductions of originals found in the house. The red stair rail 'straightens' out a wiggly wall.

LEFT **Plain Roman blinds filter light and set off the trim of the window in the smaller living room. The horse doorstop reflects the love prevailing in Kentucky of all things equine. The house is located not far from the racecourse of the famous Kentucky Derby.**

the newer half was not linked, on the upper level, with the old cabin. Separate staircases led to separate bedrooms. The owners decided to leave this arrangement as it was, so guests would be assured of privacy. Another issue was where to put the kitchen. Even though there are two front rooms, the owners did not want to cook or eat at the front of the house. They eventually decided to merge the dining room and kitchen into one cosy space in an extension to the rear of the house. This left the twin front room to function as a second, smaller living room.

The interiors were kept very simple but not primitive. Jacomini retained the spirit of the house while integrating modern conveniences, such as kitchen appliances, which share the dining room. Furnishings are select; some are old and some, like the twin pencil-post guest beds Jacomini designed, are new. Antiques, including a piesafe, an American Country storage piece, came primarily from Kentucky. Others are heirlooms from the grandmother's era – a tribute to close family ties.

ABOVE **Original to the house, the mantelpiece in the living room was stripped of layers of paint by contractor Larry Toy to reveal its leathery tone and patina. The pineapple stencil is one of several Jacomini found painted on boards, and cut and framed for the house.**

RIGHT **Twin pencil-post beds occupy the guest bedroom, where a Shaker-style pegboard links disparate windows. Jacomini painted the floor, like the pegboard and chair rail, a traditional barn red, a colour echoed in the quilts, valances, curtains and stencil.**

a sense of history

When you live in a house once owned by Louis XVI, it is hard
to ignore its grand and fascinating history. However, La Baronnie,
on the French island of Ré, is not excessively formal or imposing,
but simply an elegant, unpretentious manor house with spacious
rooms, gorgeous grounds and an air of refinement and relaxation.

ABOVE **La Baronnie has two
towers, and this is the door
to one of them, with beautiful
shutters. Outside, guests can
sit and eat a relaxed breakfast.**

LEFT **The grounds were in
as bad a state as the house
when the Pallardys bought the
property, and they have since
been completely replanted. The
huge lawn is neatly manicured
and partly shaded by old trees.**

It suits La Baronnie to be on an island, for this is a place
apart – a quiet, comfortable place, where rest and recuperation
are fostered equally by the treatments prescribed by owner
Pierre Pallardy, a dietician and osteopath, and by the beautiful
surroundings created by his wife, Florence. As soon as guests
arrive at the front door and smell the scented shrubs in the
pebbled courtyard, walk up the wide staircase and step into
their soft-coloured rooms with antique furniture and canopied,
four-poster beds, they start to relax.

Creating this haven of tranquillity was no easy task. When
the Pallardys bought the property, it was almost derelict, with
a crumbling stone façade, no water or electricity, no glass in

LEFT **The main staircase is wide and imposing, with elegant wooden stairs and an original 18th-century wrought-iron balustrade.**

RIGHT **Since it is south-facing, the kitchen is always full of light. The pine dining table and chairs are antiques, bought in St-Martin de Ré, while the blue-and-white tiles were collected, sometimes one by one, by Florence over the course of two years.**

BELOW **The kitchen is spacious but quite informal. Florence found these old glasses in an antique shop.**

the windows, only one lavatory and a badly damaged roof. This sorry sight was a sad alteration from La Baronnie's former glories. Built in the early 18th century on the foundations of a 12th-century castle, it was the manor house for the area of St-Martin de Ré and the family home of Seigneur de Beauséjour and, later, the Marquise de Tencin. So desirable was it that King Louis XVI bought it for his personal use in 1785 – although, following the French Revolution, it became national property six years later. Two hundred years later, the Pallardys were faced with the task of restoring the building authentically on a limited budget. With advice from the French authorities and help from expert architects, builders and craftspeople, they spent eight years working on it, doing as much as possible themselves until, slowly, everything came together.

At the same time as the structure was undergoing renovation, Florence was gradually designing and furnishing the interior, with the aim of creating a calm

WITH HELP FROM ARCHITECTS, BUILDERS AND EXPERT CRAFTSPEOPLE, FLORENCE AND PIERRE PALLARDY SPENT EIGHT YEARS WORKING ON LA BARONNIE, DOING AS MUCH AS POSSIBLE THEMSELVES UNTIL, SLOWLY AND DELICATELY, EVERYTHING CAME TOGETHER.

and elegant atmosphere. She decided on a palette of gentle paint shades, some copied from scraps uncovered on the old walls, and furnished each room with antiques found locally and on trips to Paris and England. The kitchen was enlarged and redesigned with a new floor and fitted wooden cupboards. A pine table and chairs from an antique shop in St-Martin de Ré harmonize with a wrought-iron light fitting, copper pans and old glassware. Most impressive are the reclaimed blue-and-white tiles, which Florence picked up over the course of two years from shops, markets and sales. Such attention to detail is typical, and has paid off in abundance with a home that combines historical accuracy with modern-day sophistication and style.

OPPOSITE **This guest bedroom is at the top of a tower and overlooks St-Martin village and the sea. Its tranquil colours are complemented by unfussy furniture and an antique quilt.**

ABOVE LEFT **Toile de Jouy makes a pretty pillowcase.**

ABOVE RIGHT **The bedroom on the ground floor of the tower has been painted a sunny shade of yellow, teamed with simple blue-and-white fabrics.**

LEFT **The panelled walls of the library were restored by the Pallardys. The style of the curtains was copied from an old painting for authenticity.**

lone star beauty

In the mid-19th century thousands of people from Germany emigrated to Texas, attracted in part by a land grant of more than 1.5 million hectares (4 million acres) secured by one Count Fisher. The German influence is still felt in many areas, including Round Top, north of San Antonio, where Tommy and Beverly Jacomini transformed a house built in 1857 by German settlers named Schramm into their weekend home.

OPPOSITE, ABOVE The informal furniture on the porch was made from tree branches. Left natural for years, the pieces were painted white in preparation for the Jacominis' elder daughter's wedding party.

LEFT The house overlooks a lake made 30 years ago. Here the Jacominis' children learned to swim; their grandchildren are now following suit.

ABOVE At one end of the kitchen is a display of baskets collected over the years by the family. A former grain barrel stores bulky paper goods, such as paper towels. 'There's never enough space in a kitchen to hold everything you need,' says Beverly.

RIGHT A tray intended for collecting berries makes a perfect carrier for napkins.

ABOVE The stencilling – apart from the roses, which were painted freehand – is original to the dining room, as is the deep turquoise of the walls. Captain's chairs also wear their original coats of blue.

LEFT The sleigh-style daybed that stands under a window in the living room is the first Texas piece Beverly bought for the house. A miniature hooked rug and a doll quilt hang on either side of the window.

OPPOSITE, ABOVE AND BELOW The old stove in the kitchen has been converted to electricity and used to display pieces of 1940s graniteware, including coffee pots that would have been used by cowboys over a campfire.

THE WILD FLOWERS KNOWN AS BLUEBONNETS ARE JUST ONE OF THE SYMBOLS OF THE LONE STAR STATE, WHERE VIRTUALLY EVERYTHING OTHER THAN THE FLORA SEEMS LARGER-THAN-LIFE. IN TEXAS, BIG IS BEAUTIFUL: BIG SKY, BIG HATS, BIG PERSONALITIES – AND BIG HEARTS.

Apart from cattle and cotton, central Texas is known for its wild flowers, including the native bluebonnets celebrated by Lady Bird Johnson, the wife of Lyndon Johnson (president of the USA from 1963 to 1969), who made it her mission to reinstate wild flowers along the state's highways.

Bluebonnets are just one of the symbols of the Lone Star State, where virtually everything other than the flora seems larger-than-life. In Texas, big is beautiful: big sky, big hats, big personalities – and big hearts. In this magnanimous state, family plays an important role. Indeed, it was family that prompted Tommy Jacomini, a Houston restaurateur, and his wife Beverly, an interior designer, to take on the rebuilding of the Schramm place, a long-abandoned house-turned-hay barn. Involving their three children in its rehabilitation would, the couple reckoned, teach them the values of home and country in a hands-on way. To emphasize their goal, the couple called their retreat the 5J ranch – for the five Jacominis.

Before starting work on the house, Beverly and Tommy had to move it from its original site in a nearby town to the top of a gently sloping hill on the 32 hectares (80 acres) of pastureland they had fallen in love with and bought for their getaway. They dug a lake fed by an artesian well to provide a focus for the

house, and they planted a stand of indigenous oaks, such as pin oak and live oak, to shade it. Trees and water would offer welcome relief from the hot Texas sun.

Tommy's father, Victor, took the role of co-contractor. Under his expert eye, local builders fitted the house with the requisite utilities, including central air-conditioning – crucial in a climate where summer temperatures top 38°C (100°F). Two deep porches and two chimneys were added to the house. Victor also stripped every door in the house back to the original pine.

Making old and new blend seamlessly was central to the redesign. For Beverly, this was when the real fun began. Slowly but surely, she and Tommy decorated the rooms and filled them with functional Texas pieces that could withstand the wear-and-tear of everyday use. Many of these were discovered at the famous local Round Top antiques fairs. All in all, it took the family a full five and a half years before they were able to move into the house, and ten in total to arrive at the look they wanted.

Three decades later, with their children grown up and married – and with four grandchildren adding to their numbers – Beverly and Tommy Jacomini can finally relax and survey their wild-flower-dappled fields with well-deserved pride.

AS A DECORATOR, BEVERLY WANTED TO EVOKE THE PAST AS WELL AS TO MAKE SURE THE ROOMS WELCOMED FRIENDS AND FAMILY IN WHAT SHE CALLS HER 'NO-RUSH' STYLE.

LEFT The daughters of the family once shared a room distinguished by matching quilts in the Grandmother's Flower Garden pattern. A framed cot quilt hangs under the air-conditioning vent.

RIGHT AND ABOVE Mementoes of Tommy's family, including his uncle's flying goggles and a portrait of his grandfather, grace this bedroom. 'All the boys have been pilots,' Beverly says. Even grandson Thomas, aged 3, is 'mad for planes'. For this reason, the 5J Ranch has its own landing strip.

LEFT The grey stain on the vertical planks that shelter the entry porch was 'manipulated' to look old, Nancy Braithwaite says. The wreath was twisted and coiled so that individual branches radiate outwards as if by centrifugal force.

RIGHT Boxy exposed posts and beams add drama to the living room. The fireplace wall was built out to match the dimensions of the antique mantel; the stone forming the hearth was also cut so that it aligned perfectly. The rug is made of seagrass.

INSET RIGHT Unable to find the ideal table for the dining room, Braithwaite had one built, then painted it red with black undertones, and distressed it to achieve an aged effect. Reproduction comb-back Windsor chairs were also painted to look antique.

highlands fling

In many regions of the USA, especially the South, summer drapes itself over the landscape like a wet flannel. When temperatures soar and humidity descends, people escape the suburbs and cities in droves, heading for the beach, the woods, the mountains – anywhere where.they can find relief from the relentless heat. Two decades ago, Highlands, a scenic hamlet in the southern Blue Ridge Mountains of North Carolina, offered cool respite to the owners of an inherited country cottage.

Founded in the 1870s by two frontier-town developers who saw the benefits of its uniquely attractive situation, Highlands has long been hailed as a healthy retreat. From its winter nucleus of 2,000, the town grows more than tenfold in summer and autumn, in part due to its proximity to the Nantahala National Forest and the Great Smoky Mountains National Park, as well as to the fabled Blue Ridge Parkway and the Appalachian Trail, which draw countless visitors to the area.

It was to this beautiful setting that Atlanta-based interior designer Nancy Braithwaite was invited by long-time friends to transform a 1970s-era generic dwelling built by the wife's father into a restful, dignified retreat. Braithwaite produces work in virtually every style, from 'French provincial to contemporary,' she says. Like her clients, though, she has long entertained a passion for American Country, so renovating the cottage in the country style was not an ordeal for her—or them.

Nancy Braithwaite is renowned for her respectful sense of place and her subtle sense of colour. To create 'place' in this house and lend it architectural definition, she turned to a colleague, architect Norman Askins. Askins was responsible, for instance, for the muscular network of whitewashed beams and posts that transects the living room. Creating this open armature imparts a barn-like sense of authenticity and history to the room. It also gives the impression that the room was opened up from smaller, cramped spaces – an illusion that makes the room appear larger and more inviting. The aura of welcome is reinforced by a hefty fireplace, made of large blocks of slate. The fireplace, and the chimney wall behind it,

ABOVE **An antique English oak plate rack highlights, among other things, a prized collection of pewter plates and tankards which the owners have assembled over the years. The two yellow pie plates are French. The bandbox on the table is wrapped in birch bark.**

RIGHT **Braithwaite designed linen-upholstered seating in the sitting room to be slightly overscaled, which augments the feeling of homely comfort. Wall-to-wall carpet, in muted grey, visibly softens the room.**

RIGHT In the master bathroom is a unique washstand (and matching mirror) fashioned from fir slabs 2.5 cm (1 in) thick.

BELOW A chequerboard of blue and white tiles runs under the clawfoot bath, a relic that had to be re-enamelled. The outside was spray-painted in one of Braithwaite's signature hues: 'blue-grey-green'.

OPPOSITE, ABOVE A pair of shelves has been fixed to a three-boarded panel that attaches directly to the wall.

OPPOSITE, BELOW The pencil-post canopy bed in the master bedroom was designed by a local artisan, Phil Ledford. The striped fabric is an overscaled version of traditional mattress ticking. To the left of the bed stands a blanket chest; to the right is an antique cricket table – so called on account of its splayed legs.

were both specially designed to showcase an antique mantel Braithwaite found and brought to the house. To lend the rooms a further patina of age, she employed a subdued palette in a signature set of colours she defines as 'dusty, ambiguous hues': tobacco, taupe, grey-green, stonewashed denim and charcoal. 'I don't like colours that jump out at you,' she says. 'Instead, I prefer it when colours change in different lights, so that you have to look at them over and over again.'

The initial renovation and decoration of the house was so successful that the owners found themselves spending more and more time there, finally deciding to make the cottage their permanent home. This decision prompted a second overhaul of the house, including a new kitchen and screened porch. Their collection of family heirlooms and antique furnishings, though – and Braithwaite's subtle colour palette – remained the same.

pretty in pink

A house in Herefordshire was the last thing that Louise Robbins expected to buy. A series of happy accidents, however, meant that she ended up with a property that suits her down to the ground. Dating back to the 17th century, it is in a picturesque Quaker hamlet with stunning views and a pretty apple orchard. Inside, charming antiques and accessories, simple but sophisticated fabrics and soft paint colours make it a beautiful, restful and perfectly ordered home.

OPPOSITE, ABOVE The house overlooks a cultivated garden filled with cottage-garden plants such as foxgloves, roses and alliums. Herefordshire houses are traditionally painted black and white, but Robbins was given permission to paint hers a delicate pale pink.

OPPOSITE, BELOW Ducks, hens, a cat and even a pair of donkeys co-exist happily here.

ABOVE The house dates from 1672, and was partially rebuilt in the 19th century.

LEFT At the back of the house is a cider-apple orchard.

When Louise Robbins came upon her house in Herefordshire, it was love at first sight. She had been looking for a property to buy somewhere between Wales and the Midlands, but had never considered Herefordshire, and was sent to view the place by chance. 'I walked through the door and I adored it from the very first moment,' she recalls. 'The way everything happened was a miracle.'

Timber-framed, with pantiles and slates, the house was built in 1672 and partly rebuilt in the 19th century. It is sited in a Quaker hamlet, overlooking apple and pear orchards and with lovely views of the Black Mountains. It even has its own orchard at the back, with a wooded copse and a cultivated garden at the front. 'It's mind-blowingly beautiful,' says Louise Robbins, who has always loved period properties, and now has her own business as an advisor on period homes and gardens – everything from interior and garden design to

ROBBINS STARTED WITH A PALETTE OF REDS AND OCHRES, WITH SOME LIMEWASHES ON THE STONE WALLS. THE LOOK IS SIMPLE BUT SOPHISTICATED, AND VERY BEAUTIFUL.

ABOVE Robbins collects Victorian printed pottery, and adores this heavy design.

LEFT The garden room looks through to the sitting room; the former is painted in Farrow & Ball's Fowler Pink, the latter in Fox Red. Robbins found the 18th-century dresser in an antiques warehouse and bought the settle at auction. All the doors in the house are, like this one, generously wide.

RIGHT The 19th-century Scandinavian pine seat came from an auction in Wales. The curtain material is old chintz.

restoration advice and researching house histories. She also
has a soft spot for animals, and visitors to the house will meet
a friendly pair of ducks, a couple of donkeys, a ginger-and-
white cat and four rare-breed Buff Orpington hens, which are
kept in a pen made from ornamental 19th-century metalwork.

Robbins believes in authenticity, and luckily the house had
been restored with great faithfulness by its previous owners,
who had exposed all the original beams and even a tombstone
from 1774 that had been embedded in the drawing-room wall.
All Robbins had to do to the structure was to complete the
installation of the flagstone floors and restore some windows,
though she also renovated three untouched rooms – an attic
room, a breakfast room and the downstairs bathroom. As for
decorating, she started with a palette of reds and ochres, with
some limewashes on the stone walls, rather restrained and
Shaker-like in style, though in the part of the house reserved
for bed-and-breakfast guests she used a cheerful, sunny
yellow. The look is simple but sophisticated, and very beautiful.

The main feature of the interior is Robbins's collection of
antiques, which she began in childhood, developing an
extraordinarily keen eye in the process. These are antiques that
are not necessarily pristine and perfect, but often charmingly
casual, humble and unrestored – such as the iron beds she

OPPOSITE Printed pottery
makes a lovely base for a
fruit display on a window sill.

LEFT The breakfast room is
painted in Book Room Red,
and has a black-and-white lino
floor. Robbins has covered a
table with an antique quilted
bedspread. She found the tall
cupboard at the end of a farm
lane in Devon. The intricate
shelf is French, and still has
its original paintwork.

ABOVE Robbins also collects
spongeware and enamelware.
The planked cupboard was
originally an art cupboard from
a primary school in Devon –
they were getting rid of it, and
Robbins was only too happy to
take it off their hands.

has had for 20 years, whose layers and layers of paint are peeling in the most attractive way, or the 18th-century English pine dresser, which she found in an antique warehouse in mid Wales. Such wonderful finds, once in a lifetime for most of us, are not at all uncommon for Robbins, who says that wherever she lives she always ends up near a great little antique shop and some interesting reclamation yards. Best of all, though, are her instinctive hunts in all sorts of unlikely places. 'Something in my brain tells me that there's an interesting object down the lane, so I always go down the lane,' she says. 'And usually there does turn out to be something there.'

Over the years she has acquired some lovely things, from the early Georgian settle that came from an auction with straw stuffing poking out of it to the plank-fronted kitchen cupboard that she found, literally, at the end of a Devon farm lane. Even her accessories are irresistible, such as a collection of allium heads in a basket, a display of Victorian Burleigh ironstone Calico plates and a plain wreath made from rope. The fabrics, too, are old, worn and delectable. Robbins's curtains are all made from second-hand, early country house chintz, the

THE HOUSE HAD BEEN RESTORED WITH GREAT FIDELITY BY ITS PREVIOUS OWNERS, WHO HAD EXPOSED ALL THE ORIGINAL 17TH-CENTURY BEAMS AND EVEN AN OLD TOMBSTONE THAT WAS EMBEDDED IN A WALL.

ABOVE **The green-painted chest of drawers dates from about 1770. Next to it, a lovely old armchair has been covered in checked fabric, the end of a roll picked up in a market.**

LEFT **This display of blue-and-white china contains some early Copenhagen pieces, alongside a mixture of others. Some pieces are chipped, but Robbins feels that this only adds to their charm.**

RIGHT **The main drawing room is filled with an eclectic mix of country antique furniture and accessories. The walls are limewashed, and the original beams were exposed by the house's previous owners.**

cushion covers are in ticking, the throws are Welsh blankets, and the beds and tables are covered with antique quilts.

There are some ways in which Louise Robbins is not quite so traditional. Although most Herefordshire houses are painted black and white, she was determined that hers should be a pretty pale pink. It was an unusual choice, though approved by conservation experts at English Heritage. Fortunately, the locals approved, too, which she discovered when a gang of farmers turned up at her door one day and announced that they had decided to call her 'Barbie Babe' – probably a nickname unique among owners of 17th-century country houses.

OPPOSITE, ABOVE **This guest bedroom – painted in bright Ciara Yellow from Farrow & Ball and furnished with an old French bed – is among several in the huge house let as bed-and-breakfast accommodation.**

OPPOSITE, BELOW **A Georgian chest of drawers is adorned by an arrangement of dried hydrangea heads.**

ABOVE **The Redouté prints above the bed in another guest room came from a friend's antique shop.**

RIGHT **Louise Robbins has owned the iron beds for about 20 years. She loves their layers of peeling paint.**

THE ANTIQUES ARE NOT NECESSARILY PRISTINE AND PERFECT, BUT OFTEN CHARMINGLY HUMBLE AND UNRESTORED. 'CHIPS, KNOCKS AND SCRATCHES ONLY ADD TO THE ATTRACTION,' SAYS ROBBINS.

turning back the clock

It was nothing if not a brave undertaking. The starting point: a bland 1950s property without much in particular to recommend it. The aim: a 17th- and 18th-century Provençal manor house, built of antique, reclaimed stone and with all the picturesque features one would expect. Yet, somehow, the owners pulled it off. This is a tale of dreams, of daring and, most of all, of dogged determination. With a happy ending, of course.

When choosing somewhere to live in the country, it may be the place rather than the property that is more appealing. This was certainly the case for one European couple, Isabelle and her husband, who fell in love with a location – a private spot in Provence, between Mougins and Grasse, surrounded by olive groves and with open views to the coast. The house itself was a rather small and unprepossessing 1950s building, but they were desperate to have it. First, they had to persuade the unwilling owner to rent it to them; Isabelle's husband flew to Paris and convinced him that they were ideal tenants, and eventually he agreed. Later, he sold it to them and, over the next seven years, they raised their three sons there, enjoying the house despite its cramped awkwardness.

Finally, though, the time came when enough was enough, and a bold, even extravagant, plan was formed. They would transform the house from top to bottom, turning it into a typical

LEFT **In the kitchen, a simple stone sink is complemented by a curvy tap. The thickness of the new walls can be seen around the window. Like all the walls of the house, they were rendered with marble powder, which is not only washable and durable but also soft and cool to the touch. Antique pieces are displayed under the sink and on an adjacent zinc-covered work table.**

ABOVE **Simple materials and textures – stone, glass, rush, distressed wood – give this house a centuries-old feel.**

TOP **Isabelle has collected antique cutlery over the years.**

ABOVE RIGHT **A wall of cupboards lines one side of the kitchen. Isabelle found the table in a decorative antique shop near L'Isle-sur-la-Sorgue.**

Provençal manor house of the 17th and 18th centuries, but equipped with ultra-modern technology, and at the same time expanding its size two-and-a-half times.

For three years they lived in a tiny property next door while specialist builders carried out the work. The walls were made thicker and faced with bleached stone once used in the local countryside. The doorways were enlarged and doors and windows given characterful arched tops. The floors were covered with old flagstones and the walls covered in a render made from washable, durable and beautiful marble powder.

Isabelle's faithfulness to the authentic look she wanted to create knew almost no limits. A lifelong collector with a knack of finding desirable things in unlikely places and an inherent

LEFT Pale colours unify the simple living space, from a pile of bleached stone balls to coral and a worn and faded old door, which has been simply propped against the wall for decoration. The overall impression is one of softness and harmony.

RIGHT Antique doors featuring lovely mouldings front the bedroom cupboards. Linen sheets and cushions in toile de Jouy cover the bed.

BELOW This 18th-century decorative commode is a rare piece. Isabelle fell in love with it at first sight and finally managed to buy it from an antique shop in Mougins called French Country Living.

sense of what would look right where, she spent all her time sourcing old building materials, windows, shutters, panelled doors, antique furnishings, kitchen equipment, lights, decorative accessories and all the other things required to turn back the clock on a 20th-century house by 200 or so years.

When she had finished, it was impossible to tell that the house was not really the ancient manor that it so resembled. 'We love the irregularity,' she says. 'And that sort of craftsmanship is something you just cannot find these days. These things are unique, a work of art.' Something which could also be said for the house itself, which has been transformed from a nonentity into an impressive home with grace, charm and its very own story to tell.

FAR LEFT Centuries-old oaks and maples shade the front of the house. The back looks onto a raised garden divided into quarters: two are reserved for vegetables and two for flowers.

LEFT The pedimented portico testifies to the original parson's interest in classical forms.

RIGHT The winter living room is dominated by a chimney wall fabricated of wide pine planks coloured red with milk paint. The door to the left of the fireplace recess conceals a bread oven.

BELOW A Scandinavian bench bed graces the front hall.

painted parsonage

In New England, simpler homes dating from the colonial era are scattered through the countryside, while dwellings of richer citizens tend to cluster in villages that sprang up around major crossroads. Many of these early American hamlets have attained iconic status; they are revered by those who live there, as well as by visitors drawn to village greens flanked by time-honoured meeting places such as the general store, the church and the post office.

Within New England, northwestern Connecticut is distinguished as a repository of particularly handsome colonial houses, as well as indigenous structures such as covered bridges, taverns and barns. One of the more imposing homes is the Parsonage, a fine example of 18th-century architecture set on a green in the hamlet of New Preston. Situated next to the village's Old Stone Church, it shares the street with a tavern that was the weekend home of fashion designer Bill Blass.

In the style of many a traditional New England barn, the Parsonage is painted not white but red. When it was bought some 20 years ago by JoAnn Barwick and her husband, it had already undergone a meticulous restoration by an interior designer who returned the millwork to its original condition.

As founding editor of US *Country Living* (and later editor-in-chief of *House Beautiful* magazine), JoAnn found in the restored Parsonage precisely what the 'country' in her heart craved: an authentic backdrop for the mix of early American antiques and reproductions that testifies to her signature style of decoration. 'At the time I was very involved in communicating the designs of the colonial era in my work,' she says. 'I felt incredibly lucky that the designer who owned the house before me had respected the skilled craftsmanship of the woodworkers who had put their heart and soul into every room.'

What clinched the couple's acquisition of the property was the barn, which had been transported piece by piece from Vermont to stand in the back garden at the corner of the main house. As soon as JoAnn walked into the double-height space

LEFT **Every surface in the barn was whitewashed to amplify the light that pours in through an oversized window on the loft level. The Canada geese decoys were found in a single sweep through a favourite antique shop. The armless seating units that push together to form a long sofa are upholstered in one of a** series of coordinating fabrics; others appear on the bed in the corner of the loft.

ABOVE **The dresser is one of the pieces designed by JoAnn after she left the magazine world and became a design consultant to the furniture industry. Its shelves set off a collection of antique bowls.**

'I WAS VERY INVOLVED IN COMMUNICATING THE DESIGNS OF THE COLONIAL PERIOD IN MY WORK,' SAYS JOANN BARWICK. 'THE PARSONAGE EXPRESSED EXACTLY WHAT I KNEW ABOUT OUR NATION'S HISTORY, ESPECIALLY OF THE POST-REVOLUTIONARY-WAR PERIOD.'

with its overhanging loft, 'I felt I was in a magical place,' she says. The couple capitalized on that feeling by adding a glass-walled summer room to the opposite end of the house. The two spaces function as light-filled bookends to the cosier rooms within the Parsonage itself.

JoAnn Barwick filled the Parsonage and barn with antiques she had collected during her travels while overseeing magazine photo shoots; these were supplemented with pieces she has designed for various furniture manufacturers since leaving the magazine business. Gifts augment the collection. Two pieces stand out: a poster she pasted onto a piece of wood, then cut out with a jigsaw to hang over the fireplace in the winter living room, and a mermaid that was given to her by a photographer friend. JoAnn always likes to find a place to swim wherever she works. Her mermaid is a testament to that desire.

ABOVE LEFT **Trim in the dining room and adjoining living room is painted deep green and red.**

ABOVE **The mermaid who swims over the old washstand may have been a weathervane. The salt-glaze pottery includes three pot-bellied jugs.**

LEFT **Painted in shades of grey accented with black, this floor mimics a floor in the open-air Skansen museum in Sweden.**

RIGHT **The sage-green sleigh bed is a reproduction. Early American beds tend to be short and are often tied with ropes, which do not provide adequate support for today's mattresses.**

relaxed elegance

In Geoff and Gilly Newberry's classically proportioned Georgian rectory, floral patterns break free from formality, their colour and vibrancy echoing the joyful freedom of the wild-flower gardens outside. However, classic English decorative restraint ensures that this is no disordered clutter, but rather an elegant home in which boldness mixes with sophistication and subtlety, providing a relaxing, refreshing environment where informal family life always comes first.

Now that minimalism has loosened its grip on interior style, it is time to celebrate colour, pattern and general abundance. This is good news for Bennison, an English company specializing in a very English product: high-quality hand-printed fabrics based on original 18th- and 19th-century textiles. The hand-drawn designs range from the quietly composed to the exotic, the riotous and the abandoned, in a multitude of soft, faded colours printed onto luscious cottons, linens and silks.

If Bennison's fabrics combine maximalism with restraint and elegance, then so, inevitably, do the company's owners, Geoff and Gilly Newberry, whose house in Norfolk manages to be both impressive and comfortable, exquisitely decorated yet a relaxed family home. It is full of gorgeous things, yet easy on the eye and totally devoid of pomp.

A classically proportioned, redbrick Georgian rectory built around 1760, the house stands in 2.5 hectares (6 acres) of

LEFT AND BELOW In the breakfast room, Bennison's Chinese Pheasant fabric trails around the walls, its slightly faded colours complementing the pale green and cream woodwork. The Newberrys used Farrow & Ball paints throughout 'because they change with the light'. Delicate French giltwood antiques add to the decorative elegance.

OPPOSITE Blowsy roses are the main feature of a squashy sofa in the drawing room. Above it is a large 18th-century Dutch painting of the Wertz family. Bold elements such as this are offset by a plain background of cream walls and wide elm floorboards.

BELOW **On the Georgian fireplace sits a collection of delicate pink lustreware: the perfect finishing touch to this very feminine space.**

MAIN PICTURE AND OPPOSITE **Holly's bedroom is a pretty mix of pink and white, with a painted iron bed setting the scene and Bennison's Daisy Chain fabric used on walls and curtains. An antique quilt, which is a perfect complement to the floral pattern, has been used as a table cover, and accessories continue the theme. The large corner linen cupboard is an antique, too.**

land and looks towards the pretty tower of an 11th-century village church. As with many a country property, the back door is used as the main entrance, while from the breakfast room French windows lead to a formal garden and lawns, and along a scythed path to unmown meadows where wild flowers flourish in spring and summer.

The Newberrys bought the rectory ten years ago as a place where they could escape from their hectic lives running showrooms in London, New York and Los Angeles, and to be near their children, Jack and Holly, who were at boarding school in the area. They knew immediately that it would provide them with the relaxation and inspiration that they needed, despite its anachronistic Art Deco-style interior. 'It simply had a magical quality,' says Geoff. Where some old houses can have an ad hoc, higgledy-piggledy character this, thanks to its Georgian symmetry and formal layout, felt calm and restful. At its heart is a central corridor, with well-proportioned, light and airy rooms leading off to the left and

THE FABRICS ARE AS INTRINSIC A PART OF THIS HOUSE AS ITS VERY BRICKS AND MORTAR. PATTERNS ROMP FROM WALL TO WALL, SOFA TO CHAIR, CURTAIN TO CUSHION, BED COVERING TO TABLECLOTH.

OPPOSITE Walls and curtains in the master bedroom are in matching fabric – Bennison's Tulip Tree in pink and green – while Trincomalee has been used for the sofa. Frilly-edged cushions add to the impression of comfortable abundance.

ABOVE LEFT The exquisite painted chest of drawers, acquired from an antiques dealer, is French.

ABOVE RIGHT The impressive canopy bath came with the house. The other fittings in the main bathroom are suitably monumental, including a large metal towel rail and a sumptuous double basin.

RIGHT Antique taps and a marble panel create a period feel in the bathroom, which has an exotic floral wallcovering of Bennison's Shangri-La fabric.

right. Even though some period features were missing, there was still an overriding feeling of balance and restraint.

Not much needed doing structurally, but the Newberrys did remove a small room that had been built into a landing, and extended the kitchen over two adjacent potting sheds. They replaced lost details such as fireplaces and cornices, and put in new flooring. The hallway had its original York stone floor, but elsewhere they introduced wide-plank elm, a pale golden colour that reflects light without looking showy. They used Farrow & Ball paints, a light blue and green for woodwork, with cream shades on the walls, and added furniture that complemented the interior – good-quality,

ABOVE LEFT AND RIGHT **This guest bedroom is furnished with dark-wood antiques, and a worn-leather tub chair sits in the window. To complement the elaborate walls, covered in Bennison's Pondicherry linen print, the curtains are a plain stripe; all the furniture is spare in outline and elegant in style.**

LEFT **The chic four-poster bed is a reproduction of an American Confederate style. The bedcover is an antique appliqué and patchwork quilt from the late 18th century.**

OPPOSITE **On the guest bedroom's desk are a 19th-century harvest jug filled with roses and a brass oil lamp that has been converted to take electricity. The curtains are Bennison's faded blue and red Malabar stripe.**

relatively simple antiques, some of which had been inherited, some bought at auction, and some brought back from trips abroad or picked up from dealers or shops.

It was all planned around the fabrics, which are as intrinsic a part of the house as its bricks and mortar. Patterns romp from wall to wall, sofa to chair, curtain to cushion, bed covering to tablecloth. Sprigs, buds and full-blown blooms twist and trail their way around in a profusion of flora and even sometimes fauna. But the Newberrys have inserted plains and stripes enough to ensure that the eye is entranced but never overwhelmed. This is fresh rather than fussy, classic rather than cluttered. 'We tried to create a typical English country house feel – laid back, comfortable and elegant,' says Gilly. 'There were certain fabrics that we wanted to use, so everything followed from there.' The transformation took two years, but now they have a house that suits them perfectly, a retreat with wild meadows outside and a lavish country garden inside that never needs watering or pruning.

rustic

Quirky and time-weathered, rustic homes are often set at a remove from urban civilization; indeed, their owners truly want to get away from it all. These are homes that speak with the gutteral dialect of a long and intensely personal history. They bear the scars of habitation with pride, while relinquishing nothing of their hardy spirit. To the casual eye, rustic houses may seem rough, but it is this very ruggedness that appeals to their owners, who share a pioneering appreciation for apparently unpromising spaces characterized by an abundance of wood and stone. Idiosyncrasies abound: consider the rakish roofline and doorways of the Crooked House, the ancient converted barn, the hull-shaped timber framing of a coastal retreat and the remote restored watermill. All testify to the ecological sensibility that underlies a comfortable rustic look.

the crooked house

Looking out over the wooded valley of the River Lugg in the Welsh mountains, the Crooked House lies at the end of a short, rough track. It consists of a 16th-century cruck-framed building merged — in fine Celtic harmony — with a two-up-two-down 17th-century timber-framed cottage and an 18th-century barn.

LEFT AND ABOVE **A quirky haven of peace in the rolling Welsh hills, the Crooked House glories in its unique vernacular architecture, which the owners are determined to preserve. The house is painted in a mix of whitewash and a pigment known locally as raddle.**

With a roof that resembles a wild switchback of two-tone tiles and corrugated iron, the Crooked House could have come straight from a fairytale by Hans Christian Andersen. For the couple who bought it some 25 years ago, it was what they had searched for long and hard. Their philosophy was a simple one, formulated with the help of some searching questions. Why pillage an old house just because you have become its owner? Why not just let it be, let it stay in the shape it has taken over time? What, they asked, is restoration all about? Can one not adapt one's needs to the building? Surely, having

ABOVE In the wood-framed part of the house, built in the 17th century, flaking whitewash tinted with natural pigment covers original wattle-filled walls, oak beams and doors

TOP The main parlour in the 17th-century cottage has a comfortable mix of 17th- and 18th-century oak and fruitwood furniture. Everything in this room remains in regular use.

LEFT AND ABOVE RIGHT The 19th-century kitchen has been left much as it would originally have been, with pine and beech table and chairs. The set, dating from the same century, was made nearby and came from a local house. The floor and steps, carefully looked after by the present owners, show evidence of years of wear and tear. An old grain chest is still used for storage.

stood this long, with its crooked windows, crazy roof and a list to starboard, the Crooked House must know best. In flight from the 20th century, with its fixtures and fittings, stresses and conformities, the owners welcomed the house's old-age cracks, eccentric character and wonky lines. When they arrived, sheep and a handful of cows were gently grazing within its derelict walls; there was no water or electricity, and daylight was visible through the many cracks and gaping holes in the roof. But they were undeterred.

With their wish to preserve rather than rebuild, they retained the flagstoned 18th-century kitchen standing in the timber-framed cottage part of the house. This kitchen is dominated by a huge fireplace with a spit-rack, a pivoting 'sway' for holding

LEFT, RIGHT AND BELOW The guest bedrooms, which have singularly sloping floors, are in the wood-framed section of the house. Here, parts of the original wall construction are on view. The beds have feather mattresses placed on taut ropes – an arrangement that gave rise to the saying 'sleep tight'. To get a firm mattress – and a good night's sleep – you had to tighten the wooden pegs holding the ropes.

ORIGINALLY SINGLE-STOREY, THE HOUSE NOW HAS TWO AND, IN PLACES, THREE STOREYS, REACHED BY FIVE STAIRCASES – OR SIX, IF YOU INCLUDE THE LADDER LEADING FROM ONE OF THE GUEST BEDROOMS TO THE ATTIC ABOVE.

cooking utensils and, high above the fire, a smoking rack that sits in its original slots. A door leads to the parlour with some original wattle-and-daub wall panels and limewashed walls and ceiling. Next door, in the part of the house that contains the oldest piece of timber – a cruck beam, smoke-blackened from the open, central hearth that once burned here – stands a 19th-century kitchen, complete with restored bread oven and working cast-iron range. And next to that is the 20th-century – though hardly high-tech – kitchen, where the fridge is clad in elm planks, a Rayburn oven cooks the meals for the paying guests and heats the water, and where the 'sink' consists of a slate milk cooler 2 metres (6½ feet) long.

On the first floor, as well as a bathroom, are three bedrooms with feather beds, including a fine four-poster. Duck under the cruck in the master bedroom, and you reach the 'red sitting room' above the dairy, the two forming a wing added in 1984.

Work on the Crooked House is hard and never-ending, but it is a labour of love. The result is a unique, welcoming home that bears its age proudly, boasting to the world of its survival.

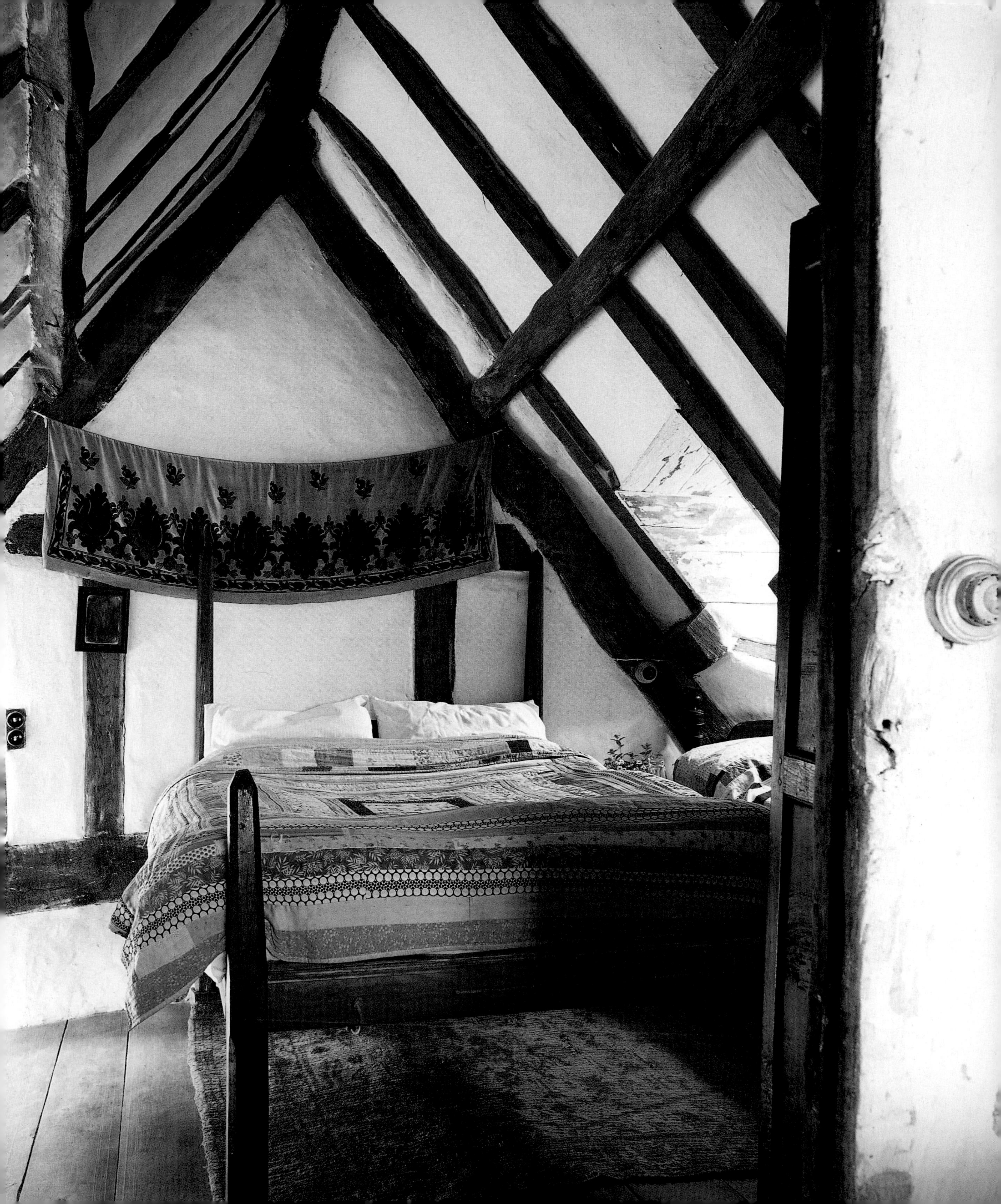

home on the range

The 'Biggest Little Town in Texas' is actually one of the smallest, with a resident population of just 81. Settled in 1826, Round Top became a mecca for German immigrants. One of them, Victor Witte, arrived from Hanover in 1872. After claiming land for his family, Witte built a three-room farmhouse for his son, Armin; his granddaughter lived there until 1967, when it was bought by Virginia and Robin Elverson. They called it Walnut Hill Farm.

ABOVE AND OPPOSITE, BELOW The cookhouse was built of square-cut pine logs held together by cement, stones and mud. Over time, the bond deteriorated and was replaced by a plastic version, which 'gives' with the weather.

OPPOSITE, ABOVE The pickets on the back porch appear to 'shimmy', or vibrate; Virginia says that the idiosyncratic touch is 'typical of fences in this part of Texas'.

Even though it is too small to appear on a national road atlas, Round Top – located in the heart of Texas, north of San Antonio – has achieved fame by hosting one of the largest and most celebrated antiques shows in the USA. The Round Top Antiques & Folk Art Fair, held on the first weekends of April and October, attracts thousands of visitors. But, even before the fair became well established, the Elversons (and interior decorator Beverly Jacomini, whose farmhouse is featured on pages 32–37), among other country-starved souls, had already fallen in love with the area and decided to put down roots there.

When the Elversons took possession of the 162 hectares (400 acres) that comprise their property, they, like many others in the area, leased the land to cattle farmers. Over the years, they also made a number of personal

changes. Armin Witte had already moved an 1853 barn onto the farm; several log cabins were also in place, including one near a big pond at the back, which the Elversons use as a dressing room when they go swimming. Armin's niece added two rooms and a porch to the farmhouse before the First World War. To accommodate their own family, the Elversons converted one of the rooms into a bathroom, and attached another log structure to the house by means of a passage; this became their winter living room.

The Elversons and their two teenage children joined forces to renovate their home. 'It became a family project,' Virginia says. 'The kids loved it.' Among their tasks were painting and stencilling the bedrooms. Scraping off layers of paint from the planks that sheathed each room, they unearthed Witte's original colour palette. Virginia checked these against the

VIRGINIA ELVERSON BECAME AN EXPERT AT EARLY AMERICAN HEARTH COOKERY AND GAVE DEMONSTRATIONS OF TRADITIONAL DOMESTIC SKILLS TO SCHOOL GROUPS AT THE BLACK WALNUT KITCHEN TABLE.

ABOVE Simple triangle brackets support shelves, which hold an array of antique blue-glass preserving jars and a white ceramic mould. A wire egg basket, bought from an old café, folds up into itself on a nail alongside.

RIGHT AND LEFT Installing a window on either side of a store cupboard let sunshine into the dark old cookhouse; whitewashing the interior and painting the ceiling blue between the beams also helped to enhance the light.

colours in a nearby museum of domestic life. 'I went over with my watercolours and matched all the colours that would have been true to the 1870s,' she says. The family softened the pinks, yellows and blues they found so that the new paint would give the appearance of being weathered by time.

Virginia's favourite structure is an 1850 log cookhouse. Even though it has no electricity or water, Virginia, an author of two cookery books, became expert enough at early American hearth cookery using period tools to teach school groups these skills using the cabin's massive stone fireplace.

Thirty-five years on, cattle no longer graze the land, which is gradually returning to its natural state – its cedar, oak and elm trees attracting the return of wildlife. Even so, Walnut Hill Farm remains 'central to our life', according to Virginia. 'We are lucky that way.'

AFTER RESEARCHING THE COLOUR PALETTE THAT WOULD HAVE BEEN USED IN THE 1870s, THE FAMILY SOFTENED THE PINKS, YELLOWS AND BLUES THEY FOUND SO THAT THE NEW PAINT WOULD APPEAR TO HAVE BEEN WEATHERED BY TIME.

ABOVE RIGHT **The Elversons stencilled the bedroom behind the living room with a pattern incorporating swags, Indian paintbrush plants and black walnuts – reflecting the name of their farm, Walnut Hill.**

LEFT AND RIGHT **Virginia says that her husband, a former British RAF officer, wanted 'to save everything Texan' in the house. Living room 'saves' include a pine storage cabinet called a piesafe, a spool daybed used as a sofa, two rockers and a doughbox next to the faux-grained front door.**

jewel in the mountains

Recycled timber, a traditional design and local wood carving create a feeling of great age in this modern family house in the Swiss Alps. It was planned as an escape from busy city life and the owners knew just what they wanted: a traditional-style chalet full of light and shadowy corners, rich colours, old furniture, the smell of beeswax and fine antique rugs. The result is a stunning home with extensive views over the village and the mountains, and with a seasoned appearance that belies its recent construction.

ABOVE The chalet provides exhilarating views of the village of Verbier and the mountains. In summer, it is surrounded by a carpet of wild flowers.

OPPOSITE, ABOVE In common with architectural styles in many parts of the world that suffer from long, cold winters, window areas have been kept small to help with insulation.

OPPOSITE, BELOW A table is set for a meal on the main veranda – a wonderful spot to languish in summer or winter – where the high quality of the intricate wood carving can be fully appreciated.

The site chosen for the chalet was Verbier, in Switzerland, a village the prospective owners knew and had come to love from many family holidays spent there. They and their four children had outgrown the chalet that they used to occupy. Something larger and better suited to their needs was now required.

Traditional Swiss chalets do not pop up on the market every day of the week, so to achieve what they wanted, they decided to build a new one, using recycled old timber. Without further ado, the plot of land next to the chalet they knew well was acquired, and a local architect was commissioned to draw up the plans. This venture was to be a maiden voyage for both architect and owners. He had never before been asked to produce a chalet-style house from traditional materials; they had never built a house from scratch.

LEFT, TOP AND ABOVE RIGHT
The living and dining rooms occupy one large area on the first floor. The living area is dominated by an open log fire and the floor is covered by a richly coloured kelim. Most of the furniture in this room consists of old French pieces, but the dining chairs are from an English chapel. A built-in bench under the window provides additional seating.

ABOVE **The cosy feel of the chalet extends to the kitchen, with hand-painted wooden cupboards and Mexican tiles behind the oven. Copper pans, brass handles, woven baskets and a butcher's block continue the rustic theme.**

The result is breathtaking – a family home with space for everyone and incorporating a longed-for library – with beautiful views over the village and the mountains, and with an age-old appearance that is the fruit of much research. Although Verbier is now an attractive village, and a well-established part of the tourist trail, until some 30 years ago it was neither pretty nor prosperous. The farmhouses that were built there were on a rather modest scale and, unlike those of wealthier Swiss communities, lacked a uniform style. So the architect turned to the 200-year-old chalet style of the neighbouring Val d'Iliez for his inspiration – and this outstanding home with its carved wood, low ceilings, small windows and Val d'Iliez green shutters was born.

TRADITIONALLY, THE GROUND FLOOR OF A SWISS CHALET HOUSED THE ANIMALS,
THE FIRST FLOOR WAS FOR HUMANS, AND THE TOP FLOOR, WITH VENTILATION
HOLES UNDER THE STEEPLY SLOPING EAVES, WAS FOR STORING WINTER FODDER.

This new home retains the traditional
three-storey construction of a Swiss chalet.
Its ground floor, built from local stone, is
the children's area, housing their bedrooms
and bathrooms. In winter, the family uses
an entrance on this level, which has a highly
practical concrete-floored 'mud room' for
muddy boots and skis.

The remainder of the house is built of wood,
with traditional carving by craftsmen from the
nearby Val de Bagne. The summer entrance
is on the first level, which has a brick-floored
kitchen, the library and a large living and
dining room, plus a huge balcony that wraps
itself around one whole side and three-
quarters of the front of the house, and which
can be reached from the kitchen or the living
room. The master bedroom suite and two
guest rooms are situated on the top floor,
with a small balcony leading from the master
bedroom. Overhanging it all are the wide
eaves of the traditionally constructed wooden
roof, providing shade for the balconies
beneath when the sun reflects off the snow in
winter or when it floods in during the glorious,
wild-flower-studded summer months.

OPPOSITE **Verandas were constructed all around the original building to create a series of sheltered, semi-outdoor rooms at ground level, while on the upper level each bedroom gained an outdoor platform to allow occupants to take full advantage of the beautiful views.**

RIGHT AND FAR RIGHT **All over Seagull House, maritime ephemera and reminders of the coast are positioned to reflect its waterside location.**

a work of art in wood

BELOW **The family may have up to ten boats on the creek at any one time, for sailing or enjoying a relaxing session on the water.**

Seagull House was once an undistinguished 1950s block – but that was before architect Roderick James arrived with his family, drawn to the far southwest of England by the house's position high above a tidal creek in Devon amid lusciously wooded valleys that climb steeply from the water.

Roderick James is an architect who has been in practice since 1974 working on oak barns. He was interested in Seagull House not only as a family home but also as a place to talk to clients and demonstrate what could be done with wood and building techniques that have been practised in England and Wales for more than seven centuries.

Transformed from the featureless block that the James family took on in 1988, the house now consists of the original building encased in wooden cladding, clinker-built for a fine nautical effect and enlivened by a ground-level veranda and a first-floor balcony. There is a new, full-scale timber-framed 'barn' using trusses, beams and joints developed in England before 1300. Between the two is a single-storey link that houses a studio for Roderick's artist wife Gillie. This building is also covered with wooden cladding and, like the other two, roofed in slate. The three enclose a courtyard garden planted with ebullient greenery. The entire complex fits snugly into the surrounding woods.

The result is a rambling, complicated sort of building with enormous variety in its spaces and angles. None of the rooms rivals in drama the great expanse of the barn, which is not divided into rooms except for a gallery. It is stabilized by huge braced collar trusses and the focal point is a fireplace of near-brutalist concrete. There is neither a ceiling nor any attempt to hide the beams and braces. The floor is pale wood, as is much of the furniture, while sofas and chairs are covered in plain colours. Natural light pours in from roof lights.

The wide balustraded balcony provides wonderful vistas of the nearby water and woods from the bedrooms of visitors and the

RODERICK JAMES WENT BACK 700 YEARS TO FIND A TECHNOLOGY THAT IS JUST AS ELEGANT AND ADAPTABLE AS THE HIGHEST-TECH BUILDING OF THE 21ST CENTURY. HE CHOSE MEDIEVAL TIMBER FRAMING.

ABOVE The glass walls of the dining area would, in medieval times, have been filled with wattle and daub. In the 21st century, glass gives far more light and exploits the views.

LEFT Dozens of storm lanterns hang in the mud room. They are put out to light the way to the house for parties on dark nights. It is a practice in keeping with the waterside setting, where lights have been used for centuries to guide and cheer fishermen and sailors.

RIGHT The main living room resembles the inside of a boat's upturned hull. It is constructed with timber framing – a craft pioneered in England 700 years ago and now enjoying a revival.

family alike. Nearly 2.5 metres (8 feet) above the ground, it runs round the entire area of the original house and every bedroom opens onto it. The rooms' French windows are glazed and painted a soft sea blue, and there are comfortable wooden American chairs for lounging during open-air summer breakfasts and siestas. In winter the same walkway offers the chance to spot migrant shorebirds.

In Seagull House you will find model yachts in bathrooms and bedrooms and given prime position at the end of the dining room. There are decoy birds everywhere, too – wild ducks, geese, snipe and sanderling.

James is very proud of his nautical blood, which may explain why he feels so at home working with wood and water. 'My forebears were sea captains, the owners of barques and brigantines. I have a genetic link with the sea, and have always had boats.' He still has them – no fewer than six can be seen from Seagull House, moored across the creek.

WOOD IS USED IN A WAY THAT RECALLS MARITIME BUILDINGS AND SHIPS' CABINS. BEDROOMS AND BATHROOMS ARE PANELLED WITH ROUGH-SAWN HORIZONTAL PLANKS AND THE JOINTS ARE FILLED WITH A PAINTER'S CAULK OF SOFT WHITE.

OPPOSITE AND ABOVE **An enormous 19th-century family portrait turned out to be just the right size to fit, floor to ceiling, in this inviting guest bedroom. The simple iron bed, painted white, is covered in one of Gillie James's quilts, whose sandy colours with splashes of blue pick up the muted decorative theme of the rest of the room. Above the head of the bed are a couple of the family's old model yachts, now collector's items.**

RIGHT **One of the spare bedrooms has this nautically themed bathroom en suite. The walls are made of very roughly sawn boards, with marine caulk used in between. It is like being in an old wooden ship.**

RIGHT **Surrounded by dense plantings of oak and Judas trees, vines, ferns, roses, lilies and clematis, the buildings sometimes appear submerged in the abundant growth.**

LEFT **Natural materials have an affinity and sympathy with each other. Here, chunky clay pots and a simply constructed wooden porch sit comfortably with the stone mill buildings, achieving a timeless grace.**

the sounds of silence

While our ancestors may have longed to leave behind the simple rural life, for us it is often a luxury to return to a materially impoverished – but spiritually rich – environment. The link between the paucity of material comforts in a place and the enjoyment to be found there is particularly pronounced at this remote riverside hideaway in France. For its fashion-designer owner and his friends it is 'heaven on earth'.

It was only by happy accident that the current owner discovered a ramshackle watermill and adjoining barn deep in the countryside of southwestern France. The location is about as far from his home and professional life in Paris – both physically and mentally – as he could get while remaining on French soil. Set in a lonely clearing, the early 19th-century buildings are 10 kilometres (6 miles) from the nearest village and several kilometres from any other dwellings.

The converted mill has been simply furnished. 'The fact that the buildings originally had a practical, functional use means I have a lot of freedom to live here the way I want,' says the owner. 'I like empty spaces around me so the layout is totally open-plan, and consequently the views from inside are wide-ranging. I have not decorated the interiors, just put in country furnishings and large pieces of furniture whose simplicity appeals to me.' Although the watermill hasn't operated for more than 25 years, for 11 months of the year the water still

ABOVE **The blue paint used inside and out is a traditional colour linked with the wood treatment** *bleu charette* **– a paste created in the production of woad, once commonly used as a dye in Europe. It is not only beautiful to look at but also a natural insect repellent.**

RIGHT **Enjoying the fact that the original buildings were not designed for human habitation, the owner has chosen minimal decoration and furniture that is appealing on account of its rural simplicity.**

RIGHT AND BELOW LEFT
AND RIGHT **The barn, like the
watermill, has been simply
furnished and decorated in
accordance with its functional
origins. A palette of white, grey
and soft blue has been used on
the mismatched woodwork to
create a harmonious effect that
does not look over-contrived.**

courses under and next to the mill, creating 'a serene rocking impression' and
acting as a seasonal and meteorological barometer. 'The river changes from
season to season, yet is always a strong, calming presence. In high summer it
regularly dries up to little more than a trickle. But the weather can change very
quickly; the river bed suddenly fills with water from rain in far-distant hills and
the garden can flood in no time.'

Ironically, given the lack of neighbours and the mill's distance from civilization,
socializing with friends is an important aspect of life at this haven. 'I have lots

RIGHT The guest bedroom, with its inviting patterned eiderdown, overlooks the living-room area.

OPPOSITE Distinguished by an eclectic combination of mirrors, the bathroom, like much of the rest of the mill, has been furnished with finds from the local salvage depots.

BELOW Most of the bedrooms in this unique retreat are built on mezzanine floors above the main living area. Each has the feel of a private hideaway with its own distinct character.

'THE MILL IS VERY ISOLATED AND IT'S A BIG EFFORT TO GET THERE,' SAYS THE OWNER. 'BUT ITS REMOTENESS IS A CRUCIAL PART OF THE PLACE. LIVING IN A CITY FOR MOST OF THE YEAR, I PARTICULARLY APPRECIATE THE SILENCE.'

of visitors here. Often six or so people at a time, and more for special holidays. My guests do exactly as they please – whether it's playing music, reading, chatting or indulging in long, lazy lunches. There are books everywhere and big armchairs.' Cooking is an important preoccupation and the owner loves to work in the kitchen with the doors and windows thrown open so that he can continue conversations with friends outside while preparing meals. In the vegetable patch, courgettes, peppers, tomatoes and lots of herbs are grown for the kitchen.

Given the owner's connection with the fashion industry, his desire for 'somewhere to be calm and enjoy a timetable-free rhythm', somewhere away from sophistication and formality, is quite understandable. For three months of every year he takes the opportunity to 'do nothing but look, live, cook with produce from the garden and listen to the silence and the sounds of the water running next to the house, the birds, the wind in the trees and nature all around.'

a converted barn

When Marina and Peter Hill returned to Britain after several years of living in Venezuela, they decided to settle in a rural part of southeast England, near Guildford, but they wanted more space than the average country cottage could offer. At auction, they bought a lot consisting of a barn and two outhouses.

The primary building on the Hills' site was a large barn, thought to date from around 1650. It had a sturdy timber frame and two large doors on both sides, designed to allow horse-drawn carts to pass directly through the building. The structures were in good condition but lacked proper foundations, on account of their age and historical non-residential use, so they had to be underpinned before any other construction work could begin. To achieve this, it was necessary to strip down the buildings to the skeleton frame and support them internally.

FAR LEFT AND BELOW LEFT
The barn and outhouses flank
a courtyard that in a former life
served as an animal enclosure.
Wherever possible, panels of
glass have been inserted in
the outside walls to take
advantage of natural light.

LEFT Recycled items such as
this wooden-plank door have
been installed to harmonize
with existing elements.

BELOW On the far side of the
barn from the courtyard, glass
panels have been set above a
new oak-clad door to increase
the light in the living room.

RIGHT **Double doors that once opened to admit horse-drawn farm carts have been replaced by an expanse of glass that gives a sense of continuity with the central courtyard and enhances the feeling of spaciousness.**

BELOW **Directly linked with the more formal dining area is an airy, spacious kitchen and breakfast room, created from one of the outbuildings.**

OPPOSITE **Inside the main barn is a mezzanine TV room overlooking the open-plan living space. Broad, shallow brick steps descend from the original doorway on the right; at the near edge, they have been extended to create an imaginative sitting area.**

Although the barns had been sold with planning permission for conversion to domestic use, and architectural drawings were available, Marina Hill decided to ignore these and develop the building herself. Decisions evolved gradually, she says, about how the space should be divided to suit her and her husband's lifestyles and to accommodate their collection of large South American paintings.

While the main structural work was being done, the couple moved into one of the smaller buildings, so Marina was on site for most of the building work and could be directly involved on a day-to-day basis. The conversion of the main barn took a year and a half to complete. It now has an open-plan living space with a sitting area around an open hearth. A mezzanine balcony has been erected from recycled timber that was specifically chosen to be in keeping with the original beams. The beams were themselves treated for woodworm before being sealed with a wax finish.

One of the outbuildings was transformed into a wing consisting of bedrooms and bathrooms; the other is now a spacious kitchen and breakfast room with large windows overlooking the central

ABOVE White paint has been used throughout the barn conversion in order to offset the potentially darkening effect of an abundance of wood.

RIGHT AND ABOVE RIGHT Decoration has been kept simple and subdued in order to accentuate original features. White walls emphasize the old beams in these two bedrooms.

LEFT Streamlined bathroom fixtures, dominated by chrome, white stone and ceramic, have been chosen to harmonize with the rustic setting.

COLOURS HAVE BEEN KEPT DELIBERATELY LIGHT AND SIMPLE, AND MATERIALS HAVE BEEN SELECTED FOR THEIR EARTHINESS AND SIMILARITY TO EXISTING ELEMENTS – MANY ARE RECLAIMED OR RECYCLED, CONTRIBUTING TO THE WELL-BLENDED MIX OF OLD AND NEW.

courtyard. Planning restrictions limited the type of windows the Hills could install, so they had to make maximum use of light that could be obtained through doorways. And, as a public bridlepath runs close beside the outer wall of one of the bathrooms, the window there had to be obscured to maintain privacy. The old barn doors leading onto the courtyard have been replaced with fixed glass panels, allowing plenty of light into what was previously a dark space. The doors on the other side of the barn have been extended beyond the original ones to reach ground level.

Marina says that the buildings had a 'dignity of their own' that she wanted to maintain. Her decorative scheme was devised to accentuate rather than diminish the original features. Among the many interesting elements she introduced was a bucket sink set into a concrete surround and finished with a Philippe Starck tap. This brings together the utilitarian feel with a touch of modern classic design, epitomizing the way the converted barn appears today.

LEFT **Simple chairs, baskets, painted enamelware and gingham fabric complement the house's unpretentious style. The pendant light is made from an inverted terracotta pot.**

RIGHT **The stone farmhouse is more than 300 years old, and was just two large rooms when Bauer bought it. The external staircase is the ideal place for a potted-plant display, while a pedestal table has been set up in front for informal meals in the sunshine, shaded by a canopy of climbing plants.**

outdoor living

Taking an ancient uninhabited farmhouse and turning it into a cosy place to live was no great challenge for Diana Bauer. She simply got on with the job, despite having little money to spend on the restoration. Her informal, inexpensive solutions are utterly charming and entirely appropriate to the style of the property, which is now as much a base for relaxed outdoor living as it is a comfortable, unfussy family home.

Long, leisurely days spent lazing in the sunshine of southern France. Informal meals on the terrace, shaded by a canopy of trees. An abundance of plants clambering over old stone walls, with terracotta pots lining the steps. Beautiful views over olive trees, vineyards and woodland. All this might sound like an idyllic dream, but for Diana Bauer and her family it is a glorious reality.

Bauer has owned her 300-year-old Provence farmhouse in a quiet medieval village for 45 years and, understandably, she still adores it. It is a tiny property which, when she and her husband bought it, had one room for the owner to live in downstairs, with a bed in a niche in the wall, a large room for storing hay upstairs, and a place to keep a horse outside. Though charming, and typical of the region, it had been uninhabited for 50 years and needed a great deal of work to turn it into a viable home. 'We were too broke to do anything much,

LEFT AND INSET LEFT A rustic lunch has been set up in a shady corner, with canvas and wicker seats, comfy cushions and mismatching crockery.

RIGHT Large glass doors lead straight from the kitchen into the garden, letting in abundant light and allowing the family to come and go easily. Plant pots on the step bring the outdoors almost into the house.

BELOW Floral-patterned china complements unfussy striped fabric. Bauer had no particular scheme in mind when she chose the furnishings for the house; she just wanted to keep it as simple as possible.

and anyway we wanted to change it as little as possible,' says Bauer. 'Our rule was to keep it simple.' They renovated the masonry, installed an internal staircase, created a kitchen/dining room and a sitting room downstairs and put a washing machine in a nearby toolshed. Upstairs they created three bedrooms, one very small (ideal for a child), and a bathroom.

'The rest just came by itself,' explains Bauer. 'We already had most of the furniture we needed and there was no great decorating scheme.' Their mantra of simplicity, simplicity, simplicity is evident everywhere, showing how informal, low-cost solutions work well in such a setting. Limewashed walls complement the original tiled floors and beamed ceilings, and the furniture is delightfully mismatching, though coordinating in terms of its plain, comfortable style. Kitchen storage spaces are hidden by gathered panels made of Provençal fabric. The

bedrooms have rag rugs, old American quilts and unobtrusive window treatments, with open bookshelves, patterned cushions and paintings dotted around the walls.

During the summer the family spend their time almost entirely outdoors, coming and going through the kitchen's glass doors and choosing a different place to sit each day, while in the winter they eat outside as often as possible. The house is cool in summer and cosy in winter, says Bauer, but most of all it is incredibly comfortable and peaceful. There is nothing pretentious here – what you see is what you get – yet it is perfectly functional, captivatingly pretty, and entirely fitting as an inside–outside family home.

ABOVE The large niche in the wall of the sitting room, now a cushioned seating area, was where the former owner once slept. A palette of whites and pinks creates a calming space.

LEFT The beamed bedroom, with its traditional tiled floor, has limewashed walls, a rag rug and gathered curtains on the plainest of poles.

OPPOSITE, ABOVE The knotty, grained, wooden cupboard doors in the kitchen are totally unpretentious, as are the mismatching, wicker-seated dining chairs.

OPPOSITE, BELOW At the other end of the kitchen, hooks for hanging everyday utensils have been banged into the wall. The gathered panels that disguise storage space have been made from traditional Provençal fabric.

romantic

A fanciful, sometimes winsome mood pervades the romantic home, revealing an attitude to country living that is at once ingenuous and sophisticated. Without standing on ceremony, these lovingly tended abodes – whether found in a fishing village in Denmark, the sleepy Cotswolds or a hilltop village in southern France – gracefully bare unabashed artistic souls. None succumbs to the merely sentimental; each hints at a sweetness of spirit that is endearingly heartfelt. Romantic houses also express dreamy yearnings for a simpler age when manners mattered. They respect their forebears, even as they adapt to contemporary needs. Frequently bathed in a limpid light and caressed by a pastel palette, romantic rooms are filled with pretty, feminine furnishings marked by a delicacy of silhouette. Such rooms inspire relaxation and intimacy. They are cosy indeed.

coming up roses

There is much beauty to be found in simplicity, and Jette Arendal Winther's house on the north coast of Zealand in Denmark is nothing if not simple. It is a humble fisherman's cottage, and she has taken her lead from its restrained style and held back from too much interference, just adding muted paint colours, plain fabrics and attractive old furniture that she has transformed into charming additions to this individual and irresistible home.

RIGHT **Taking down the door opened up the space between the dining room and living room. Arendal Winther found both the bench seat and the wardrobe in a flea market; the latter was very plain until she decorated it. On the table are two examples of her pretty décollage ceramics.**

ABOVE **Even the garden tool shed is picturesque.**

Like many artists, Jette Arendal Winther is inspired by her surroundings. For years she lived in Copenhagen with her musician husband Niels, but six years ago the couple decided that urban life was too expensive, particularly since they needed to maintain not only a home but two studios as well. They had friends in the fishing village of Hundested, an hour's drive away on the north coast of Zealand, and had visited the area many times. So, when a friend found this little cottage, they didn't hesitate. 'We came and looked, and bought it the next day,' she says.

Since then, Arendal Winther has never looked back. 'I'm inspired by being in the country,' she says. 'The things I make now I could never have made when I was in the city.' Her current work, mainly bowls, dishes, teacups and other tableware, is romantic and graceful, using the découpage technique of cutting out decorative images, pasting them

onto glazed and fired pieces and then firing
them again – though she prefers to call it
décollage, since it combines transfers with
flowing brushstrokes for its distinctive effect.
The images chosen might be mythological
or theatrical, but they are frequently floral,
coming directly from her garden, which is
rambling and wild.

When Arendal Winther moved in, the garden
was a total mess, uncultivated and overgrown.
She and Niels have spent a great deal of time
creating new beds and planting old roses and
other traditional species, though there is still

RIGHT **The original kitchen was left much as it
had been, except that Arendal Winther removed
some wall cupboards and replaced them with
her own colourfully patterned hand-made tiles.**

OPPOSITE **The white gloss-painted floors offset
the timber of the old French dining table and
chairs. The chandelier adds a fanciful decorative
touch; Arendal Winther found it in a flea market.**

ABOVE LEFT **The fisherman's
cottage is in a sleepy village on the
north coast of Zealand, Denmark's
main island; it has wonderful views
over the harbour and out to sea.**

ABOVE RIGHT **A subtly coloured
old schoolroom map dominates the
dining room, which is decorated in
Arendal Winther's characteristically
laid-back rustic style.**

much to do. The house, on the other hand, has been easier to tend. Built in 1941, it is a timber-framed fisherman's cottage, filled with light and with views over the harbour and the sea. In terms of decorating, they took their lead from the house's style, preferring minimal intervention to overperfection.

One change they did make was to paint the outside of the house a pistachio green with dark green woodwork. Inside, they stripped off the wallpaper and painted the walls in muted shades of green and umber. They covered the wooden floors with tough, shiny, marine paint to reflect the light, and in the old kitchen took some cupboards off the walls and replaced them with Arendal Winther's hand-made tiles, leaving everything else as it was.

The biggest job was to build a small studio extension. It has a stone floor, huge windows, plain white walls which offset the owner's colourful ceramics and an ever-changing noticeboard pinned with inspirational images. Much of the furniture is plain wood painted in

ANY PRETENTIOUS OR EXPENSIVE FURNITURE WOULD STICK OUT LIKE A SORE THUMB, SO ALL THE PIECES ARE RUSTIC AND HUMBLE, OFTEN FROM FLEA MARKETS OR JUNK SHOPS.

LEFT About a year after they moved in, the Arendal Winthers built a small extension to accommodate a studio for Jette. It is a simple room, with a stone floor, white-painted walls and huge windows. On the wall she pins a constantly changing selection of images which inspire her work.

ABOVE AND RIGHT Arendal Winther's ceramics are made by a découpage technique, in which she cuts and pastes small decorative images onto the pieces. Now that she lives in the country, her style has changed totally, and she is very influenced by the old roses that grow in her wild garden.

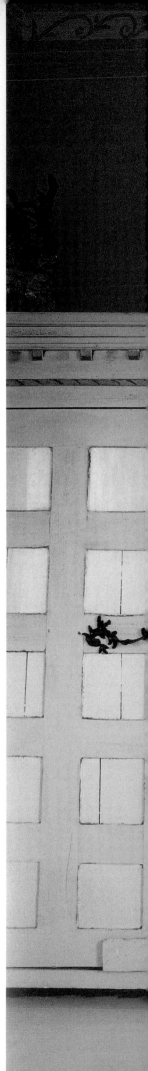

LEFT Arendal Winther's sister is a painter, and the picture on the wall of the sitting room was a gift from her. The old wooden bench seat was found in a flea market; it has been made comfortable with some plump cushions and pretty throws.

RIGHT The 18th-century Danish linen cupboard is another find of Arendal Winther's, which she painted turquoise and white. The room in the background, where an old metal bed serves as a sofa, is her husband's studio, and doubles as a guest bedroom.

BELOW LEFT The style of the house is utterly simple and unpretentious. All the furniture, accessories and curtains are humble in origin, though as good-looking as can be.

THEY PREFERRED MINIMAL INTERVENTION TO OVERPERFECTION. 'THE HOUSE FEELS HARMONIOUS,' SAYS ARENDAL WINTHER, 'AND WE HAVE BEEN SENSITIVE ABOUT REDECORATION. WE DIDN'T WANT TO INTRODUCE TOO MANY MODERN THINGS.'

pastel colours, especially blues and greens. Each piece is rustic and humble, often from inauspicious beginnings such as flea markets or junk shops, but transformed ingeniously to become a useful and beautiful addition to the home – like the old iron bed, covered with a rose-printed quilt, which serves as a sofa, or the sewing-machine stand turned into a bedside table by the addition of a top made of tiles. Fabrics, too, are simple, from curtains to cushion covers, either plain or restrained florals that she buys from a market stall.

As is evident from the look of the house through and through, Arendal Winther's great skill is to identify the potential in something that others might overlook and to give it a new lease of life in her inimitable, imaginative style.

OPPOSITE **The building was originally two farmworkers' cottages. When the Thorntons moved in, with their bantams, they put up a blue picket fence around the garden.**

RIGHT **Melanie Thornton has, over the years, assembled a large collection of beautiful blue-and-white spongeware from the mid 19th century.**

FAR RIGHT **Thornton found the Somerset dresser on one of her buying trips. Its colours coordinate with the striped curtains and cushions made of old fabrics from trade fairs, auctions and dealers.**

BELOW **The utility room is charmingly unsophisticated but perfectly practical.**

calm and cosy

Carefully chosen antiques and a variety of well-loved old textiles fill this 200-year-old Cotswold cottage with relaxed character. Owner Melanie Thornton aimed to combine the pretty and the practical, using natural materials and a palette of pale, calm colours as a backdrop. The result, straightforward and unfussy, is also warm, cosy and very appealing.

An ideal country house combines beauty with practicality. 'It must be a livable, usable space,' says Melanie Thornton, an antiques dealer and decorator. 'You can have pretty touches, but you've got to be able to put your muddy boots in the hall, too.'

Thornton's former home, a 200-year-old stone cottage in the Cotswolds, epitomizes these traits. When she moved in, it had a bland 1970s, semi-open-plan interior, and her aim was to make it feel cosy and mellow, while being robust enough to take whatever was thrown at it. It was a gradual process, involving use of natural, local materials as far as possible. She and her husband added a laundry-room extension, for example, using old Cotswold stone roof tiles and a salvaged

ABOVE **Old linen and cotton pillowcases, with intricately embroidered detailing, look superbly comfortable.**

RIGHT **The antique patchwork quilt was bought at Newark antiques fair. The wardrobe doors were made to fit an alcove in the bedroom, and old handles were added.**

OPPOSITE, ABOVE **A guest bedroom in the attic looks highly inviting. Thornton adores old textiles, and she collects little dresses such as the ones hung on display.**

OPPOSITE, BELOW **Plain furniture from the mid 19th century suits the style of the house. A colour palette of blue and white keeps the main bathroom pretty and simple.**

window, and finished it in lime render. When they replaced the yellow plastic kitchen with one made by a friend from old pitch pine, they used a reclaimed sink and draining board, laying flagstones pulled up from a nearby pub. Thornton painted the walls of the cottage with natural milk paints that had to be mixed up in a bucket, all in shades of off-white, from chalk to stone to ivory.

The furnishings were chosen to suit the house, mostly country antiques from the mid 19th century, which are typical of Thornton's laid-back style. An old Cornish dresser displayed most of her crockery, and a school cupboard held the food. A 1930s sofa, which she had re-covered, was a gift, and the soft furnishings were all made from fabrics she had collected over the years. When finished, it was undemanding, unfussy and unselfconscious, easy to live in and enjoyable, too – just as a country house should be.

moving on

This 18th-century farmhouse has seen many changes. It has been a dilapidated wreck, a cluttered family home, and a funky, brightly coloured space. A few years ago, Lena Proudlock transformed it into a cool, calm and collected Swedish-style residence, full of light and a feeling of utmost serenity, using pale colours and simple furniture and subtly imposing a sense of order.

OPPOSITE, ABOVE **A Georgian farmhouse with beautifully proportioned rooms, the building was in a sad state when Lena Proudlock bought it. It needed extensive building work, from rewiring to the rebuilding of staircases.**

OPPOSITE, BELOW **The original elegant Georgian staircase has survived. When Proudlock had to add another staircase to the second floor, she had it copied.**

ABOVE **The sense of simplicity and calm comes from a strictly limited colour palette, careful use of plain furnishings and no frivolous extras. The fireplace came from Proudlock's former house, and the French mirror over it was found in an antique shop in the Chilterns.**

RIGHT **Garden chairs were brought indoors to create an unusual and striking feature in the sitting room.**

LEFT The beautiful old dresser was already in situ when Proudlock bought the house. However, she had to take out an awkward staircase from the kitchen, and lay new floors, which were painted white to reflect plenty of light.

RIGHT Cupboards were put in to match the dresser, and an Aga was installed to replace a range cooker that no longer worked. The wall light came from a junk shop in Oxford.

BELOW These dining chairs, copies of Swedish Gustavian originals, are from Proudlock's furniture collection.

Lena Proudlock is irrepressible. A textile designer who produces a range of denims in 60 glorious colours, she designs elegant Swedish-style furniture and is a portrait photographer, too. She also makes a habit of doing up houses – so successfully that they are often used as backdrops for magazine photo shoots – and runs a business letting out her houses for luxury weekend breaks. If all this sounds impressive, it seems even more so when you know that it followed a near-disaster about 12 years ago, when she was on the brink of bankruptcy and had to sell a huge mansion that she had been living in for years.

Looking urgently for a new home, Lena Proudlock saw this late 18th-century farmhouse advertised for sale in *Country Life* magazine. Realizing that it was just down the road from her current property, she immediately jumped into her car and went to look at it. 'It was empty, so I just pushed the door open and walked in,' she remembers. 'I was stunned. From the outside, it looked like a two-up, two-down cottage, but an extension had been added at the back and there was an attic room that ran the entire length of the house.'

Proudlock was lucky enough to buy the house at auction, but then began nine months of hard work, because the house needed extensive renovation. In the kitchen, she knocked out a staircase and a wall, removed an old range and installed the Aga from her former house. She added three bathrooms, raised the beams in the

attic, replastered the walls, put in some wooden floors and painted them, rewired, replumbed, and replaced the doors and windows in several rooms.

Proudlock decorated with a mixture of Farrow & Ball historic colours, rush matting, pretty curtains and cluttered furniture. 'But after five years I improved it,' she says. She tore up the carpets, removed the curtains and most of the furniture, and repainted the walls in lilacs and blues. The result was a cool, calm Scandinavian look with lots of light. 'I loved that Nordic look and got passionate about the colours,' says Proudlock. It was also a turning point for her, in that she then decided to design her own furniture to fit the rooms. She complemented her designs with pieces from car-boot sales, auctions and antique shops, and used only plain, checked or striped fabrics.

But it was only a matter of time before Proudlock changed everything all over again, injecting bright colours for floors, walls and furniture. And, more recently, she bought another house nearby, which is decorated in black and white, with crystal chandeliers and giant plasma TV screens. The thrill of moving on, of experimenting, is what keeps Proudlock going. And keep going she does, because stopping is not an option.

SHE TORE UP THE CARPETS, REMOVED THE CURTAINS AND MOST OF THE FURNITURE, AND REPAINTED THE WALLS IN LILACS AND BLUES. THE RESULT WAS A COOL, CALM SCANDINAVIAN LOOK, WITH LOTS OF LIGHT.

LEFT **The walls of the main bedroom are painted in Mirabel Blue by Coles, offsetting the wide elm floorboards, which are original to the house. The four-poster bed was one of Proudlock's first furniture designs. Draped over it is some old French ticking, found on one of her regular hunts for interesting pieces.**

ABOVE **The runner, dating from the 1930s, is Swedish.**

RIGHT **Proudlock's home office is typically sparse and serene, with minimal furnishings and fabrics. She painted it in French Lilac by Sanderson.**

LEFT A gallery of artwork by the Arbuthnotts' children and friends decorates the hall. The chair on the left was found in the attic of their first house, painted and re-upholstered to look better than new.

FAR LEFT The wooden bergère between two windows in the kitchen was bought at a sale. The checked blanket and plump cushions make it cosy.

BELOW LEFT The symmetrical hall has a staircase at each end. The iron balustrades were made by a local blacksmith. Vanessa Arbuthnott designed the fabric on the chair seats.

RIGHT The planked front door was specially made to replace an agricultural sliding door.

natural harmony

It is hard to grasp the unpromising origins of this lovely property. Once a cowshed and two piggeries, it has been converted – with enormous care and sensitivity – by owners Vanessa and Nick Arbuthnott, a fabric designer and architect. Indigenous, reclaimed and natural materials were the key ingredients of this harmonious home, which successfully mixes classic style with easy practicality.

Despite its spaciousness and elegance, the Arbuthnotts' house exudes friendly informality. The two staircases, for example, have been used as goalposts in many a game of football, while the kitchen is the 'everything room', where the family spend most of their time, usually surrounded by children's paintings drying on a clothes line.

When they were renovating the house the four children were all under six years old. 'It was a race against time,' says Vanessa. 'We slapped on the paint and used furniture we had already, just mending things where necessary.' This description belies the hard work that went into transforming what had been an 1890s cow byre and two piggeries.

RIGHT All the bedrooms were created in the roof space of the old cow byre, so they have pretty, sloping ceilings. The Arbuthnotts' impressive sleigh bed is the fruit of ingenuity – when their old bed broke, they cut off the base and hammered on two shaped ends made of medium-density fibreboard.

BELOW The Arbuthnotts fitted woollen carpet upstairs for its softness and warmth. The fabric on the armchair in their bedroom is an old French linen.

OPPOSITE, ABOVE AND BELOW With a wood-burning stove at one end and an Aga at the other, the kitchen is where Vanessa, Nick and the four children spend most of their time – what Vanessa describes as their 'everything room'. Appropriately for a former cow byre, the name of the pale yellow paint colour is Hay.

For over a year, the Arbuthnotts depended on a generator, and initially they had no internal doors, but gradually the house took shape. Nick is an architect who specializes in renovating old farm buildings using traditional styles and natural materials. He designed a home that kept as much as possible of the original structure, re-using materials where feasible and adding new elements with sensitivity. He created a hallway, a study, the kitchen and a studio for Vanessa, who designs hand-printed fabrics, and added five bedrooms in the roof space.

All this was carried out, says Vanessa, with the aim of 'keeping it indigenous, and not terribly expensive – we look like a humble farm building that has been here for years'. And so, with mismatched, mended furniture and Vanessa's informal fabrics, the house eventually came together as a family home.

LEFT **Kuentzmann-Levet collects antique books; although this is not as old as some she has, it is a beautiful gardening book dating back to 1914.**

BELOW **The greenhouse is an informal jungle of plants in a mix of zinc and terracotta containers, together with tools, cloches, baskets, seed trays, watering cans and other paraphernalia.**

OPPOSITE **A casual outdoor dining area is surrounded by a collection of antique ironwork, including a small cage from Provence that was once used for hunting thrushes, and a candle chandelier. The square wooden planter matches the country-style back door.**

where time stands still

This converted Normandy barn opens onto the garden from every aspect – so, with its high ceilings and pale paint colours, it is full of light and a feeling of airy spaciousness. Only an hour's drive from Paris, it is so peaceful that it might as well be cut off from the outside world – a place that time simply forgot.

For French stylist Annie-Camille Kuentzmann-Levet, authenticity is everything. She has a passion for the 18th century, and while she adores antique furniture and curiosities such as birdcages and gilded wooden columns, she dislikes with a passion reproductions and false painted decoration. She values the attraction of the original, the hand-made irregularity and centuries-old patina that cannot be achieved by today's modern manufacturing methods.

It took Kuentzmann-Levet three years to find her perfect country home, but eventually she fell in love with a 19th-century barn in a village only an hour's drive from Paris, on the border of the île de France and Normandy. The L-shaped house is built of stone and brick, with exposed beams and unusually lofty ceilings

– more than 5 metres (16 feet) high in places. It stands in the middle of a large garden, with gravel paths winding through flower beds, an orchard and a vegetable garden. Outside the living/dining room is a south-facing courtyard, where roses and old vines clamber around an arbour. Every room opens onto the garden via French windows, so that the house is full of light. A smaller stone building nearby serves as Kuentzmann-Levet's studio.

It might be a peaceful haven now, but when she arrived the garden, in particular, needed a great deal of work. It was unkempt, with too many weeds and large trees. She set to work tidying and reorganizing it, while at the same time rationalizing the inside of the house. The ground floor consisted of one large, open-plan space, with the kitchen leading directly off the living area. By building a wall with a reclaimed 18th-century door, she separated the kitchen, adding understated wooden cupboards

KUENTZMANN-LEVET HAD THE TERRACOTTA FLOOR TILES IN THE KITCHEN COPIED FROM THE ORIGINALS, AND USED BRICK-LIKE, RECLAIMED TILES ON THE WALLS – THEY ARE THE SAME AS THE ONES USED IN THE PARIS MÉTRO.

LEFT The huge living and dining room has south-facing French windows, all with pale grey, gathered curtains. The two-part cupboard, called a *buffet à deux corps*, is early 18th century and holds a collection of antique china. The elegant armchairs, known as *chaises à la reine*, date back to the reign of Louis XV.

ABOVE In the kitchen there is a combination of new and 18th-century tiles, both with a blue-and-white pattern.

RIGHT The kitchen was once part of the open-plan ground-floor space, but Kuentzmann-Levet separated it off with a wall and an old door.

WALLS, BEAMS AND WOODEN CEILINGS WERE PAINTED WHITE, TO MAXIMIZE LIGHT AND OFFSET THE OWNER'S COLLECTION OF PAINTINGS AND HER FURNISHINGS, MOST OF WHICH ARE IN THE CHARACTERISTIC 18TH-CENTURY COLOURS OF GREY, GREY-BLUE AND DARK RED.

ABOVE LEFT The warm red bedroom curtains complement antique textiles. The Louis XV boutis, or quilt, is a chintz in the *indienne* style, folded on top of a 19th-century bedcover made from a petticoat.

ABOVE RIGHT A Louis XV chaise sits at one end of the living room. The cupboard has been painted a bold *sang de boeuf*, or bull's blood, colour.

RIGHT The guest room has a Directoire bed with Polish-style curtains and a Louis XVI toile de Beautiran bedcover.

OPPOSITE The bathroom is furnished with an antique clawfoot bath and a 1930s basin with old copper taps.

painted in grey-blue, antique wall tiles and terracotta floor tiles. She also built a mezzanine area to serve as a guest bedroom, and put in a bathroom with a clawfoot bath, canopied by a Louis XVI frame of gilded wood which – ingeniously – closes to become a shower. Walls, beams and wooden ceilings are painted white, to maximize light.

The furniture dates almost exclusively from the Louis XV and XVI eras, and includes some fabulous pieces such as the double cupboard displaying antique china, and a pharmacist's bookcase holding part of Kuentzmann-Levet's collection of more than 600 18th- and 19th-century books. However, while some pieces are grand and impressive, others are more modest in style. There are no strict rules here about provenance or expense, simply a firm belief in the appeal of authenticity.

OPPOSITE **Light flooded into the sitting room through the original arched windows.**

RIGHT **Chintzy china suited the look of laid-back comfort.**

FAR RIGHT **In the back sitting room, where a window seat was strewn with cushions covered in old fabrics, new panelling made from medium-density fibreboard was fitted. It looked as though it had been there for centuries.**

BELOW **The back hallway, lined with coats, shoes and boots, led to a family room occupied by an old-fashioned rocking horse.**

a wreck restored

This is a story of an ugly duckling that became a swan. Derelict and unloved, a 19th-century former stable block was in desperate need of renovation – and Ali Sharland and her husband were brave enough to take it on, devoting two years to creating a cosy, relaxed home, full of casual old furniture and pretty fabrics.

When Ali Sharland bought her Cotswold home ten years ago it was, quite frankly, in a mess. Built of stone in 1840 as a stable block, it had been converted into a home in the late 19th century, but had much later been turned into five student bedsits and, more recently, allowed to become completely derelict. Nevertheless, the potential of the house was obvious – not just from its size and structure, but also because of its position, halfway up a hill, overlooking a village and valley, so that every night twinkling lights lit up a marvellous view.

'We had to do everything,' recalls Sharland, who has since moved house again. 'We had to take out and put in staircases, knock down internal partitions, rewire, replumb and put in a new kitchen and bathrooms.' The process took two years, during which time the Sharlands camped out in the house, moving from room to room as the work went on. Fortunately, the property had some further redeeming elements, not least of which were the original early Victorian features which had,

ABOVE **This vintage printed cotton, which Ali Sharland brought home from her shop, made a perfect tablecloth.**

RIGHT **The wooden kitchen was put in by the Sharlands at the time when the house was renovated. With its pale floorboards, cream-painted units and open shelving, it was the epitome of simple country style – even down to the antique bone-handled cutlery.**

RIGHT A new Aga cooker was installed in the kitchen, backed by reclaimed blue-and-white tiles.

BELOW LEFT A simple old slatted-wood table by the window was a great place for growing potted herbs.

BELOW RIGHT Sharland deals in decorative antique furniture from France and England; the house was full of lovely pieces such as this country chair.

ALI SHARLAND USED OLD FABRICS - LINENS, TOILES, FLORALS AND GINGHAMS - TO MAKE CUSHION COVERS, CURTAINS, BEDCOVERS, BLINDS AND TABLE LINEN. NOTHING WAS TOO WELL MATCHED, PRISTINE OR FUSSY. IT WAS JUST A MATTER OF PRETTY FABRICS MADE UP IN SIMPLE WAYS.

amazingly, been left untouched, such as the arched windows in the sitting room and the wide wooden floorboards, which Sharland restored. To complement the period style, she put an Aga in the kitchen, surrounded by reclaimed blue-and-white tiles. She also installed reclaimed cast-iron column radiators, and fitted panelling to the walls of the back sitting room which, though made of plain and inexpensive medium-density fibreboard, was extraordinarily effective.

Much of the furniture in the house was either antique or from second-hand shops. 'It was all a bit thrown together,' says Sharland. 'After doing the structural work, we didn't have much money left for decorating, so it was largely a question of painting the walls and woodwork and making the best of the furniture we had.' Most of the paints came from the ever-popular Farrow & Ball range, in soft, typically country-house colours, though in the front sitting room they opted for a polished-plaster effect in cream.

At the time, Sharland was on the verge of opening her shop, Sharland & Lewis, in nearby Tetbury, which sells English and French decorative antiques and vintage textiles, and furnishing the house was something of a trial run. 'I didn't plan it, it just sort of happened,' she says. 'But the house was very easy to live in.' Plan or no plan, that seems like just the way anyone who loves laid-back style would want their home to be.

ABOVE **Ali Sharland's shop also specializes in beautiful old monogrammed linens.**

LEFT **Most of the windows in the house had seats. Simple curtains and cushions made from Sharland's collection of fabrics made this a good place to sit down and read a book – or simply relax and do nothing.**

RIGHT **A wardrobe was built into this bedroom corner; its cut-out doors were lined with toile de Jouy to complement the vintage fabric on the bed.**

LEFT Even the storage rooms at La Louve have a spare and casual elegance. Pillsbury left this room almost as it was, with rough walls and floor, and a simple shelf with hooks, though she did add a Danish stove for extra warmth.

BELOW AND OPPOSITE Nicole de Vésian converted two tumbledown village houses into a beautifully simple home, retaining all the authentic features. In the garden she planted local species such as rosemary, thyme and lavender, clipped into sculptural shapes, which contrast wonderfully with the rough stone walls.

formal simplicity

The sculpted gardens of this ancient village property in Provence complement its spare, almost monastic interior. It is a work of art, says owner Judy Pillsbury, who bought the house from the woman who had spent ten years transforming it, designing every element to perfection, from rough stone walls to simple curtains, from clipped thyme and lavender to the plainest of paint colours.

It could be said that Judy Pillsbury is as much the curator as the owner of La Louve, her 17th-century retreat in Provence, since most of the house, and almost all the garden, were actually created by their previous owner, the gifted former fashion and fabric designer Nicole de Vésian. What Pillsbury has done is to take a unique property and sensitively improve a few key areas, while remaining true to the spirit of de Vésian's striking concept.

Judy Pillsbury is an American print dealer, who bought the house almost by accident. She had been looking in Tuscany, finding only expensive places badly in need of restoration, when a friend who lived in Provence told her about La Louve. She visited just once and

LEFT **A simple stone staircase dominates the main living room, its shape echoed by that of the plain bookshelf behind. The sweet little chair was given to Pillsbury by de Vésian's children; its seat and back were made by de Vésian from pieces of old tapestry.**

RIGHT **The hall floor is strewn with local river stones, linking the interior with the exterior in a basic and beautiful way. The cupboard door hides the electricity meter.**

BELOW RIGHT **Bare stone characterizes the interior, its surfaces revealing a surprising variety of textures and colours. In the entrance hall, de Vésian installed a baptismal font in which to dry lavender.**

'THERE ARE SO MANY LAYERS TO THIS HOUSE. YOU HAVE TO CONNECT YOUR EYE AND LEARN FROM LIVING IN IT AND THE AURA THAT IT HAS, LIKE LIVING WITH A GREAT PAINTING,' SAYS JUDY PILLSBURY, WHO WAS RELUCTANT TO MAKE CHANGES.

made an offer immediately. 'There was something so peaceful and so authentic about it,' she says. 'It was absolutely perfect.'

In the ten years that she had owned La Louve, de Vésian had transformed two tiny tumbledown village buildings into a simple, almost monastic home with a remarkable sculptural garden. The walls remained bare, often rough stone, the floors were covered with jute carpets and the windows were hung with plain fabric. Her colour palette was very strict: nothing but toning greys and beiges, and her furnishings were very modest, mostly flea-market or roadside finds. The result was something that combined a rudimentary, peasant-like feel with an innate elegance and grace.

Judy Pillsbury was, understandably, reluctant to alter such a wonderful place. 'There are so many layers to this house,' she says. 'You have to connect your eye and learn from living in it and the aura that it has, like living with a great painting.' But, aided by François Gilles and Dominique Lubar of IPL Interiors in London, she decided to introduce two further elements – a

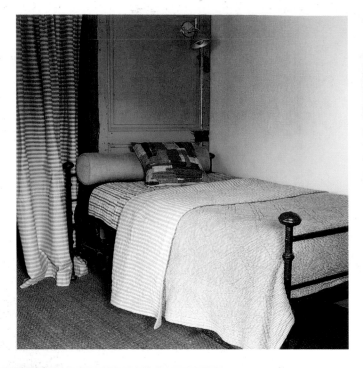

little more comfort and some soft colours taken from the local countryside. This is no place for excess, however, so the comfort is minimal and the colours muted – an old American quilt here, a Provençal boutis there. One large project that Pillsbury undertook was to make a summer kitchen from what had been an outbuilding where de Vésian dried and arranged flowers. Another was to complete the guest bedroom upstairs, adding a sink and bath, bookshelves and a sisal carpet.

In the garden Pillsbury replaced a ladder to the plunge pool with stone steps, reconstructed a stone wall and built a lap pool, and she retained de Vésian's two gardeners to keep the shrubs neatly clipped. 'She wasn't really a gardener,' says Pillsbury. 'Though the way she mixed plants and stone is extraordinary. But then, the whole place is a work of art.'

TOP LEFT **The guest bedroom is plain but comfortable, furnished with an old iron bed that Judy Pillsbury found at the local flea market. On top is a Provençal boutis, or quilt.**

ABOVE **In the main bedroom, Pillsbury and François Gilles hung gathered ticking curtains from wrought-iron poles made by a local ironworker. Pillsbury bought the armchair from a country furniture shop in Paris, and the chest of drawers from the local flea market.**

TOP RIGHT **Where the walls have been rendered, they are painted in white limewash or soft stone colours. Much of the pleasure of the house, however, comes from the bare materials, such as stone and timber, which have been left to look as natural as possible.**

OPPOSITE **The guest bedroom, once a place for pigeons to nest, was unfinished when Judy Pillsbury bought the house. She added a sink and bath, shelves, a sisal carpet, and this bed, covered in a 19th-century embroidered American quilt and a checked boutis.**

LEFT **Old crockery, glass and enamelware pieces adorn the mantelpiece. The cupboard to the right of it is an old French cheese larder from a market.**

RIGHT **The kitchen dresser, which came with the house, was repainted to freshen it up.**

BELOW RIGHT **The table is from Emmaus, a second-hand furniture warehouse. Its gingham oilcloth cover echoes the gathered gingham curtain beneath the work surface.**

chic and easy

A second home, especially in another country, can sometimes become a burden rather than a pleasure. For John and Monique Davidson, however, their inherited Normandy manor house, decorated with simple old furnishings, has proved a delightful place in which to get together with their family, relax and unwind.

John and Monique Davidson are not afraid to mix and match. Through their company, J&M Davidson, they source and sell an eclectic mix of homeware, from wool throws to toile de Jouy, from Vietnamese bed linen to pretty china, and in their bolthole in France they have followed the same line of thinking, avoiding the predictable and conventional. The house is full of salvaged furniture, junk-shop finds, family heirlooms, antiques, a few of their own products, and bits and pieces they have picked up on buying trips and holidays.

A typical Normandy manor built in the 16th and 17th centuries, the house was a family inheritance and is co-owned by Monique's sister, Michelle Bocquillon, a stylist on the French magazine *Marie France*. Michelle shares the Davidsons' innate good taste and has the same ideas as them when it comes to decorating, so there have been no rows about curtain fabrics or paint colours. Instead, the

LEFT The panelled dining room has cupboards that also open into the kitchen. Simplicity is key here; mismatching chairs have been given white linen slip covers, while the table is covered with an antique linen sheet. The room is lit by an ironwork chandelier.

BELOW LEFT A cast-iron daybed sits under the window of the dining room. It is piled high with cushions covered with toile de Jouy and ticking.

RIGHT The curving stairway leads from the entrance hall to the first floor. The elegant writing desk dates from the very early 20th century.

THE MIX OF FURNITURE, BLUE AND WHITE COLOURS AND UTILITY FABRICS HAS RESULTED IN A LOOK THAT IS PART ENGLISH COUNTRY HOUSE, PART BRITTANY, PART CARL LARSSON – WITH NOTHING TOO PERFECT. A BIT OF WEAR AND TEAR HERE AND THERE IS EXACTLY THE IMPRESSION THE DAVIDSONS WANTED.

two families (they have two grown-up children each) come and go amicably, sharing New Year and Bastille Day holidays. Luckily, the house – long and thin with two distinct wings – is large enough for everyone to co-exist without getting on top of each other.

'Decorating the house was a group effort,' says John. 'But it was no problem at all. We inherited some things with the house, brought some things over that we had in England, and picked other pieces up in France. Nothing is new – we went to the second-hand furniture warehouse Emmaus quite a lot, for example, which was great for little finds. Some of them were quite ordinary to start with, but Michelle repainted them, or we recovered them in ticking fabric, and they were transformed.'

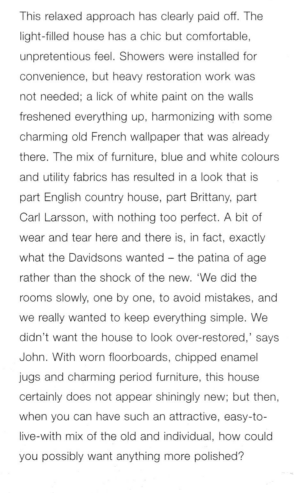

This relaxed approach has clearly paid off. The light-filled house has a chic but comfortable, unpretentious feel. Showers were installed for convenience, but heavy restoration work was not needed; a lick of white paint on the walls freshened everything up, harmonizing with some charming old French wallpaper that was already there. The mix of furniture, blue and white colours and utility fabrics has resulted in a look that is part English country house, part Brittany, part Carl Larsson, with nothing too perfect. A bit of wear and tear here and there is, in fact, exactly what the Davidsons wanted – the patina of age rather than the shock of the new. 'We did the rooms slowly, one by one, to avoid mistakes, and we really wanted to keep everything simple. We didn't want the house to look over-restored,' says John. With worn floorboards, chipped enamel jugs and charming period furniture, this house certainly does not appear shiningly new; but then, when you can have such an attractive, easy-to-live-with mix of the old and individual, how could you possibly want anything more polished?

ABOVE **The antique rolltop bath was already in situ in the master bathroom. The Davidsons love the worn look of the painted floorboards.**

TOP **Some of the rooms, such as this guest bedroom, retain their old wallpaper.**

ABOVE LEFT **The house has spacious halls and landings. White-painted walls and pale-carpeted floors create a sense of calm and comfort.**

OPPOSITE **A child's room is furnished with a pair of iron beds, and blue checked linen from the J&M Davidson range.**

simply tranquil

Houses that are simple and tranquil represent oases of calm. Embraced and soothed by their natural settings, many are located 'far from the madding crowd', so that they offer up an atmosphere of repose in landscapes as uncomplicated as they are. Graced by an aura of self-possession, these homes defer to their owners and to their sites. Consider a boathouse in East Anglia, for example, a modernistic manor in Belgium or a clapboard house overlooking a Connecticut river; all complement and pay homage to their surroundings. Inside, simply tranquil homes seem rather introspective. Typically whitewashed or painted in fog-shrouded neutrals, these sanctuaries sigh with gratitude; when colours appear, they are restrained and decorous. Wherever they may be, simply tranquil homes are congenial spaces where spirit and soul find the peace they crave.

OPPOSITE AND INSET **Set amid mature woodland, the mellow stone cottage has a tamed wildness about it. Up the driveway and across the track beyond the house lies a tranquil lake with access to more woods and walks.**

LEFT **The focal point of the entrance hall is a stunning modern table whose natural textures are accentuated at night by soft candlelight.**

timeless idyll

Anyone seeking the perfect retreat from the stresses and strains of life in the city would find it difficult to surpass this quintessentially English country cottage in Oxfordshire. Situated in a glorious rural spot, surrounded by rolling hills, ancient woods, streams, ponds and grazing animals, the solidly built stone house has provided protection and escape for a succession of owners since the middle of the 17th century.

Built of beautifully aged, golden Oxfordshire stone some time around 1640, but with some 18th-century additions, the cottage is actually two estate workers' homes knocked into one. For its present owner, an interior designer, it represented the fulfilment of a dream – but, when she discovered it, she knew instinctively that it was going to be a 'project'.

For a start, the interior – a series of small interconnecting rooms – was, for her taste, too dark, gloomy even. Without sacrificing the character that had attracted her in the first place, she needed to open it up. Though in a pitiful state, it still held the light of other days,

RIGHT When the current owner first moved into the house, the ground floor consisted of a series of dark interconnecting rooms. By exposing the beams, knocking down a wall and painting most of the surfaces white, a much brighter, more exuberant feel was created.

BELOW LEFT The old wooden floorboards had been hidden under linoleum. In keeping with the simple approach to the interior, they were stripped and lovingly polished.

LEFT Although a wall between the back and front living rooms was knocked down to make a spacious open-plan living area which incorporates a kitchen, the cottage's cosy, intimate atmosphere has been retained.

WITHOUT SACRIFICING THE CHARACTER THAT HAD ATTRACTED HER IN THE FIRST PLACE, THE NEW OWNER NEEDED TO OPEN UP THE COTTAGE INTERIOR. IT STILL HELD THE LIGHT OF OTHER DAYS – AND IT WAS THIS LIGHT SHE SEIZED ON.

and it was this light that she seized on. Now, as soon as you cross the threshold, the cottage's air of calm and timelessness is apparent. The lightness of the entrance hall and other parts of the house is achieved by a total lack of clutter and the use of simple, organic materials.

A major task was to create more space on the ground floor by removing the wall between what had been the front and back parlours. This left scope for a large living room with the kitchen at one end, but the opening-up has not robbed the ground floor of its sense of age and intimacy. The clever grouping of the furniture and the low beamed ceilings ensure that it still feels distinctly cottagey – that, plus the fact that not everything is perfect. For, although the house has been pristinely restored, the uneven walls that have witnessed life over three centuries have sensitively been left untouched.

The colour scheme is principally cream and white and, although much of the furniture is antique, the owner has

LEFT AND ABOVE RIGHT **The soothing interior theme is continued in the bedrooms, which are decorated in white with discreet hints of colour. The combination of old and new – a common feature elsewhere in the house – is also evident in the sleeping quarters. For example, in the main bedroom (left), a new bedcover has been teamed with pillows covered in an 18th-century toile, picked up from a market at St Tropez in the south of France.**

ABOVE AND TOP **With its white-painted tongue-and-groove boards, and just a touch of contrasting colour in the grey towels and dark floorboards, the bathroom is a hymn to simplicity.**

introduced several new pieces whose natural textures and colours blend perfectly with the 18th- and 19th-century oak and mahogany. The cottage is full of character and has a 'lived-in' feel, creating an overall effect that is both contemporary and comfortable.

Outdoors, the same sure touch is apparent. The spacious garden lends itself to spending most of the day outside when the weather allows – gardening, lunching or simply soaking up the charms of the countryside. Great effort was put into creating secret dells, planting flower beds, restoring the ancient wall behind the lavender beds, rediscovering the pond and opening up the streams behind their built-up, congested banks. All has been freed up and restored in the best sense of the word.

According to the owner, everything she has done came from the feel of the cottage itself. Now, after much work, she has a retreat that most city-dwellers can only dream of.

seaside boathouse

The Boathouse feels as if it could belong nowhere other than on this particular stretch of East Anglian coast. It holds centre stage in a quintessentially refined and apparently unchanging English scene, where at times the lapping of the waves and the call of the gulls provide the only hints of company.

OPPOSITE, ABOVE AND BELOW **Flanked by the ever-changing sea, and intimately affected by its moods, the Boathouse stands like a bastion between the water and the shore.**

ABOVE AND RIGHT **Despite its air of tranquillity, the location is a busy sailing and recreational centre. Surrounded by water on three sides, the house is jostled by boats of all sizes and colours, and in varying states of repair – sailing dinghies, old-fashioned rowing boats and a few working fishing boats.**

The Boathouse looks like a boathouse, but that is just a happy illusion. What's more, it gives the impression that it is about to set sail on the morning tide of the East Anglian estuary where it has stood in its present form since just after the First World War – but this, too, is an illusion. In fact, when the current owners – a couple who write and illustrate children's books – first came across it, the Boathouse was a solidly embedded part of the picturesque East Anglian waterscape. There it stood, serene in the midst of a motley collection of huts and houseboats, the centre of a sort of seaside shanty town.

On this eastern seaboard, beloved by the British royal family who, traditionally, have come here in search of healthy sea breezes, the amusements have remained gentle and decorous. In fact, the casual observer could be forgiven for thinking that nothing has happened here since about 1948.

Certainly, nothing much has happened to the Boathouse. In a previous existence, it was owned by an elderly lady with a butler and a very individualistic approach to life. The butler's quarters were in the porch, suitably curtained off. The memory

OPPOSITE **The Boathouse and its environs exude a powerful sense of the English seaside as it was in the 1940s and 1950s. In fact, it was built before the First World War but demolished during that war because it was in the way of gun defences protecting the estuary. It was rebuilt before long, but suffered damage from German strafing in the Second World War.**

THIS PAGE **The present owners have retained the distinctive ambience of the house, turning it into a refuge where comfort and tradition lend a feeling of permanence and belonging. While they were building the upper floor, the Boathouse was hit by the hurricane of 1987. Surprisingly, given that only the roof was in situ at the time, it withstood the storm.**

of this eccentric habitation lives on under its new custodians, who have, wisely, left much alone. For example, they have retained a doughty square-armed three-piece suite, together with the sentimental Edwardian prints and vases of grasses dried in coronation year (1953) in the bedroom. They have also kept the verses by Rudyard Kipling alongside words by Patience Strong on the cloakroom walls, admonishing the denizens of the Boathouse to 'Gather every shining hour'.

But they have made some changes, for instance by adding an upper floor. This is a single lookout room with windows all around. Its atmosphere is reminiscent of a sun lounge on board a pre-First World War ocean liner. For anyone sitting in one of the elegant wicker chairs, the view is of endless water, up the estuary or out to the North Sea. Since the north wind blows straight in from Scandinavia, there is a huge Scandinavian-style stove decorated with Delft tiles to warm yourself by. This room is reached by a spiral wooden staircase redolent of alpine chalets but acquired at a sale in Sussex. Under the protective East Anglian sky, the Boathouse today remains a place where Rudyard Kipling or Patience Strong would have felt at home.

LEFT In the downstairs living room with its white-painted walls, much of the furniture was inherited from previous owners. The Delft tiles on the wall behind the Coalbrookdale stove were found on a building construction site.

BELOW LEFT AND RIGHT Objects associated with the sea, particularly shells and pictures of boats, as well as nautical equipment, are to be found throughout the house.

THE BOATHOUSE IMMEDIATELY STRUCK A CHORD WITH ITS CURRENT OWNERS. THIS COMPARATIVELY REMOTE COAST, FAR FROM THE HURLY-BURLY OF CITY LIFE, REPRESENTED A PLACE WHERE THEY COULD WRITE, PAINT, WATCH THE TIDES AND SLEEP TO THE SOUND OF WATER ON THREE SIDES.

ABOVE An antique French quilt makes the bed look especially comfortable and inviting in this ground-floor sleeping nook. Known as the 'recovery room', it is the place where visiting family and friends retire to rest.

LEFT On this bedroom's walls are original photographs of the house from the 1940s. One of them has a bullet hole in the corner – a souvenir of German fire in the Second World War.

LEFT **The stone cottage is built in an L-shape, with the small garden completing the square. Louis the Lakeland terrier suns himself on the front porch.**

LEFT **The stone cottage is built in an L-shape, with the small garden completing the square. Louis the Lakeland terrier suns himself on the front porch.**

RIGHT **The cottage was once a church school, and the double doors from the sitting room to the garden occupy the original entrance, just 1.7 metres (5 foot 6 inches) high.**

BELOW RIGHT **The original double doors at the front of the house were still in situ; Smith and Moine installed the inner stable door, which leads directly into the kitchen.**

pale and interesting

Designer Mark Smith wanted a calm retreat so that he could divide his time between London and the country. When he found the perfect property – a former village school in the Cotswolds – he set about making it as light and bright as possible, filling it with appealingly plain and simple fabrics and furnishings.

When Mark Smith was looking for a country home, he did not desire a low-ceilinged, cosy cottage, preferring 'something lighter and a little bit quirky'. He and his partner, Michel Moine, spent months viewing houses, sometimes finding great places but arriving just too late or being disappointed by how dark and gloomy they were inside. The pair were on the point of giving up when they decided to give it one last try.

One sunny morning, they arrived at a stone cottage down a winding lane in the heart of the Cotswolds. At last, they had found it: a 200-year-old former dame school with a tiny garden, fields on two sides and a beautiful Norman church on another. 'I felt I had never seen anything more lovely,' recalls Smith.

Since the house was built into a slope and surrounded by natural springs, it was dreadfully damp, so the first task was to enclose the nearest spring and tank the downstairs of the property. Once dried, it was not in too bad a condition, but it needed redecorating throughout. Smith, an interior designer,

THIS PAGE **The kitchen, which leads into the light and airy garden room, has a row of antique French cutlery moulds hanging above the Belfast sink (top). The cupboards were made by a local joiner.**

OPPOSITE **Smith's aim was to open up the house to the garden as much as possible. They entertain 'not grandly, but an enormous amount – people pop in all the time'.**

had definite ideas about how it should look. 'One of the first things we did was to wash the beams with stone and off-white paints, to make it feel as light as possible,' he says. To enhance the sense of continuity from room to room, walls, doors and the staircase were clad in floor-to-ceiling tongue-and-groove boarding. The same pale colours were carried on throughout, but the spare room was painted in warmer lilac to appease Smith's sister, who refused to come and stay unless there was some colour in the house.

Smith is a great supporter of British design, and many of the furnishings in the cottage come from stalwarts such as carpet and fabric designer Roger Oates, blanket company Melin Tregwynt and William Yeoward, his former employer, who sells furniture, crystal, rugs and accessories. A local joiner made the double-sided cabinet which links the dining room and kitchen, while flooring consists of the original quarry tiles downstairs and sisal on the first floor. The soft furnishings are all made from natural fabrics such as linen, wools, ticking and old sacking, and they are plain in colour or, occasionally, with a straightforward check.

Smith has avoided anything fussy or over-ornate, choosing instead simple, unadorned pieces that do not disturb the soothing spaces he has created. 'I wanted a break from the things I am surrounded by at work,' he says. 'To clear the decks. And this place really is a sanctuary and a relief.'

ABOVE The sitting room leads directly into the garden. The generously gathered curtains were in fact very inexpensive, made from sacking fabric that fits in perfectly with Smith's plain and simple formula.

RIGHT Pale colours were used to paint the beams and tongue-and-groove boarding in the sitting room, complemented by a Roger Oates rug and a sofa covered in artists' canvas. The table is an old pig bench. 'It has lots of knife scars all over it – I dread to think what it was used for,' says Smith.

RIGHT All the bedrooms are built into the roof space, making them lovely and light. In the main bedroom, a checked blanket by Melin Tregwynt adorns the bed, and the cushions are covered in ticking. The donkey – by Steiff, of teddy-bear fame – was a housewarming present.

BELOW LEFT In the dining room a Georgian dresser is filled with a handsome dinner service that Smith and Moine commissioned from potter and neighbour David Garland.

BELOW RIGHT The garden room was converted from a derelict lean-to coal store with a corrugated-iron roof that was barely head-height. The chair is from Julian Chichester.

ALL WALLS AND DOORS WERE CLAD IN TONGUE-AND-GROOVE TO ENHANCE A SENSE OF CONTINUITY. PALE SHADES WERE USED THROUGHOUT, BUT THE SPARE BEDROOM WAS PAINTED LILAC TO APPEASE SMITH'S SISTER, WHO REFUSED TO COME AND STAY UNLESS THERE WAS SOME COLOUR IN THE HOUSE.

OPPOSITE **Near the Belgian border with France, the New England-style house, by specialist Belgian company Mi Casa, was built from solid logs with a cedar-planked stone façade. It was erected by about ten men in just three days.**

LEFT AND BELOW **The house has a roof that overhangs a porch, so it is comfortable to sit out on even the sunniest of days. Pale blue wicker chairs follow the owner's preference for being neither too modern nor too classic.**

new beginnings

This New England-style house in Belgium is striking for more than one reason. First, it is only four years old – part of a development of new, solid-wood houses, each adapted to its owner's design. Second, despite its cosy and comfortable feel, it is surprisingly modern – all clean spaces and sophisticated, contemporary furnishings. Unusual touches, however, make this a striking, haven-like family home.

For interior decorator Catherine Debal-Vindevogel, modern means not only clean-lined and sophisticated but also virtually brand new. Her house in Flanders, near the Belgian border with France, was built in a new development surrounded by fields just four years ago. Made of solid logs, with a cedar-planked stone façade, it was adapted to all her design specifications, from the number and size of rooms to the style of kitchen. 'I wanted a very functional house,' she says, 'and we use every room here. We have two children, so it has to be practical, but it is also quite minimal. I love that mix of cool and cosy.'

One of the other things that makes this house different from some country retreats is its highly restrained and subtle use of colour, pattern and surface materials. Debal-Vindevogel has chosen a palette of pale grey paints for the walls, occasionally accented with pale blue, charcoal or brown. The floors – with the exception of the flagstone hallway – are all made of oak, which has a beautiful grain, while the kitchen worksurface is an

RIGHT The house has been decorated with cool, calm colours and a carefully chosen mix of textures. As a result, it looks modern, but not in a harsh or difficult way.

BELOW LEFT Debal-Vindevogel hates clutter, so she designed plenty of storage, including this huge kitchen cupboard with wooden sliding doors. Recessed ceiling spotlights do away with the need for lots of clumsy wall or pendant lights.

BELOW RIGHT The underfloor-heating grates add to the mix of textures and materials. A lovely slab of polished stone has been used for the kitchen worksurface, its straight lines contrasting with the curvy form of the modern monobloc tap.

enormous expanse of smooth, polished stone. The fabrics are contrastingly soft, but similarly plain, in muted colours and devoid of any frills or fancies. The house gives an impression of uncluttered spaces (thanks to capacious storage which hides any mess), simple lines and calm functionality.

Carefully thought-out elements that contribute to the sleek, streamlined style of the interior include recessed spotlights that

ABOVE **Light pours into the kitchen through the floor-to-ceiling doors. The planked walls add a homely touch, in contrast to the smooth and polished surfaces elsewhere.**

LEFT **The living room flows into the dining area, which leads into the kitchen, all unified by the use of wooden floorboards throughout – though each can also be separated off, thanks to a series of folding/sliding doors.**

ABOVE LEFT AND ABOVE
**Painted a pale shade of olive, the
bedroom is filled with furniture
that has a timeless appearance.
A sliding door opens to reveal
a well-organized dressing area.**

OPPOSITE AND BELOW **With
its gilt-framed pictures, copies
of old chairs, Aubusson rug and
oversized log basket, the sitting
room has the most classic feel
of the whole house.**

take the place of wall or ceiling lights, underfloor
heating, which does away with the need for
cumbersome radiators, and the use of blinds
rather than conventional gathered curtains.

Catherine Debal-Vindevogel has chosen
furniture that is neither obviously 'modern
designer' nor overtly 'period'. Some is antique,
some new, some reproduction, but it is never dark
and heavy, though always plain and sober. The
look is chic but comfortable. Some pieces are
intriguingly different – such as the ultra-modern,
glamorously curvy, monobloc tap in the kitchen
or, by contrast, the antique, gilt-framed portrait
that hangs over the sitting-room fireplace. Such
enjoyable, individual touches give the house plenty
of the kind of character than can be missing from
some soulless modern developments. It is a place
that suits the Debal-Vindevogels down to the
ground, where they can escape the frantic pace
of their professional lives and bring up their
children in the heart of the countryside.

OPPOSITE **The renovated Victorian greenhouse is now a fabulous indoor–outdoor room, strewn with vines, nectarines and other tender plants.**

RIGHT **Boots are lined up in the hallway, while flowers tumble out of terracotta pots on the windowsill.**

FAR RIGHT **In the scullery, an old mixing bowl and a little wooden egg cupboard sit on top of a marble-topped table.**

lightness of touch

Surrounded by fields and not far from a pretty church and a moat, this Suffolk farmhouse is in an idyllic situation. And owner Eva Johnson has, in the most casual and subtle of ways, made the most of its beautiful countryside setting, emphasizing light and space with pale colours and restrained patterns, and using simple, often inexpensive, furnishings with utter individuality and unselfconscious panache.

BELOW **The kitchen occupies a room that was added to the house in the 17th century. This is 'where everything happens', says Eva Johnson.**

Patience is one of Eva Johnson's virtues, as is the ability to decorate instinctively, without trying to control the results too much. Her Suffolk farmhouse – 'a mishmash of centuries from the 15th to the 18th' – is still, she says, not quite finished after 18 years, yet to any visitor it appears effortlessly beautiful, the sort of place that just goes with the flow, without worrying about convention. 'I'm not strict,' says Johnson. 'I paint pictures as I go along, and my only aim has been to maintain the spirit of the house and to link it as much as possible with the garden. I very much believe that a house should relate to the outside.'

Since the house was dark and dingy when they first moved in, Johnson, a physiotherapist who also imports and sells the Scandinavian

OPPOSITE, BELOW **The bathroom is unpretentious and informal. The basin and rolltop bath were in the house when Eva Johnson moved in, and she scraped the paint off them to get back to the black surfaces underneath. She also installed tongue-and-groove panelling around the room.**

BELOW **Johnson tends to use very simple fabrics in informal and sometimes surprising ways. Here, the bathroom window is hung with a blue-and-white tea towel.**

RIGHT **This wooden bathroom chair was stripped, bleached and treated with oil to give it an attractively distressed air.**

OPPOSITE, ABOVE **White pebbles make a pretty still life.**

wood treatment oil Trip Trap, ripped out all the carpets and put in old pine floors, which she treated with white oil. She painted the walls in different shades of chalky off-white, to give a sense of unity from room to room. Her furniture is a mixture of junk-shop finds, antiques, some marvellous Scandinavian painted pieces inherited from her grandparents and newer things picked up here and there. Textiles tend to be made from bits and pieces found and tucked away for future use. There is no overall scheme, but her deft touch and sure eye makes it all hang together. The star of the show is the Victorian greenhouse, which she renovated and planted with nectarines and vines, and which she and her husband use constantly from early spring to late summer. This is definitely a house for living in. Or, as Johnson says, 'It's practical, and also beautiful.'

white by design

Even though the New York metropolitan area encompasses a population of 21 million, you do not have to go far to encounter leafy expanses that are as bucolic as any that are likely to be found in more remote areas of the countryside. For many who live and work near New York, Connecticut offers all the advantages of rural living at the same time as providing easy access to the city. Necklacing the Connecticut coastline, for instance, are a number of pocket-sized Edens.

OPPOSITE, ABOVE **A graceful stand of trees screens Kristiina Ratia's house from the man-made pond. In common with many of the gardens attached to well-bred properties in New England, hers is carpeted by a luscious green swathe of lawn.**

OPPOSITE, BELOW **The pond was carved out of a river 8 km (5 miles) long, providing a lovely reflective surface that bounces sunlight into the trees. The pond also functions as a buffer zone, insuring privacy for all who live on its banks.**

ABOVE **Three sturdy rocking chairs are placed on the front porch as a gesture of welcome; they are upholstered in checks from a wallpaper-and-fabric collection of Kristiina's own design. The boards on the house are unusually wide, and cut with an eccentric edge.**

RIGHT **Summer dining takes place on a vine-shaded veranda that opens onto the pool area behind the house. Kristiina combined two table bases, then had the marble top custom-made to fit.**

LEFT AND ABOVE **Kristiina converted the former garage into an all-white kitchen. She designed the marble-topped island to be large enough that children and friends could eat at it or sit with her while she cooks. French windows open onto a garden planted entirely with white flowers.**

ABOVE RIGHT **Stacks of china crockery fill every shelf. No matter how old they are, all pieces, including myriad jugs and trays, are at the ready for everyday use. None is off limits to anyone.**

Twenty-six years ago, when Kristiina Ratia and her former husband, the son of the founder of the textile company Marimekko, moved to the USA from their native Finland, they valued the convenience of city living. But that soon changed for Kristiina. Bringing up four children in a light, airy, safe environment became her priority. 'What attracted me about the place,' she says, 'was how sunny it was. It's also far from the road, which gave us a lot of privacy, so I never had to worry about the children running around outside.'

The house, a 70-year-old colonial, stands on a grassy knoll overlooking a man-made pond created in the bend of a river that leads to nearby Long Island Sound. Originally a gardener's cottage on a larger estate, the house was unusual in that it had 'a huge number of windows', Kristiina says. And it allowed for expansion – a necessity as the family grew.

The greatest change they made was to convert the garage into a bright, sunny kitchen. The ceiling opens to the roofline. Beams criss-cross the space; one of these is faux and contains recessed lights, which highlight the kitchen island. Other additions include a sitting room and a screened porch. Over time, Kristiina also updated the bathrooms, fitting them out with salvaged fixtures, which endow these spaces with character and period charm.

WHITE REFLECTS LIGHT, BRINGS OUT TEXTURES AND SETS
OFF FAVOURITE ITEMS SUCH AS BOOKS AND PHOTOGRAPHS.
IT ALSO PROVIDES A FRAME FOR FRESH FRUIT AND FLOWERS.

A former model, Kristiina is also an interior designer. In her professional capacity she defers to her clients' wishes, but her personal taste has always centred on the purity of light and space as expressed through white. The ubiquitous use of white in this instance gave Kristiina the flexibility to allow the house to go through phases. One of the rooms to benefit most from this evolution was her own bedroom, which she retires to when she wants to read in bed. She painted the floor white, hung a white ceiling fan over the bed and installed wide-slat plantation-style shutters at the windows. She also designed her bed as an upholstered island. 'I had to design it twice,' she says. 'I wanted the headboard to be the exact height of the wainscot – to lean against when I read. The first time it was too high.'

Now that her children are grown up and live elsewhere, any adjustments Kristiina makes to the house are geared to their comings and goings. 'Everything is for them,' she says. 'I'm happiest when they are home.'

OPPOSITE, LEFT ABOVE AND BELOW **A guest room has been tucked under a sharply raked eave. Kristiina added a skylight, allowing sun to pour in. Standing in for a bedside table is a traditional Finnish wedding chair – one of many in Kristiina's collection. This one is scrubbed pine; a heart is cut out at its crown.**

OPPOSITE, RIGHT **Kristiina designed the upholstered bed in her own room. From it she can wake to sunlight slanting through the shutters. The table on wheels in the window is a contemporary piece, typically used as a serving trolley.**

LEFT AND ABOVE **Both the clawfoot bath and basin in one of Kristiina's daughters' bathrooms were salvaged from a local antique shop. The bath had to be re-enamelled, and new fittings – including a hand-held shower – were attached to conform with modern plumbing. Towels are stored in the open, on hooks or on the chair next to the basin. The oversized armchair is clad in white denim.**

RIGHT **The lavatory has its own niche for privacy. Floors here, as everywhere upstairs, are painted a lustrous white.**

RIGHT **Most of the fabrics used in the house are from the Roger Oates collection. This crimson linen provides a splash of vibrant colour.**

BELOW **Slat-back, folding chairs are used for dining. The interior colours are mostly natural wood, with a backdrop of neutral walls and flooring.**

OPPOSITE **In the sitting room, the original floorboards simply needed sanding and staining.**

modern comfort

Country style does not have to mean floral patterns and antique furniture. In their Georgian home near the Malvern Hills, Roger and Fay Oates have mixed plain colours and simple, sophisticated designs to create a relaxed space that is neither overtly urban nor particularly rural – just the epitome of effortless good taste.

Roger and Fay Oates find it hard to explain how they arrived at the attractively laid-back decoration of their Georgian home near the Malvern Hills. 'We don't think about how we do it,' says Roger. 'We just do it.' The couple are renowned carpet designers (their signature striped stair runners are hugely covetable) and they also sell relaxed and elegant fabrics. Contrary to the popular image of designers, they suffer from no trace of pretentiousness, stuffiness or uncomfortable formality. 'We have always just wanted to have things we like around us and to use them,' says Roger. 'It's a question of getting your priorities right.'

The 18th-century property, a former pub with a cottage attached, is a classic Georgian design, well proportioned and with great views

over an apple orchard towards the Malverns. The couple bought it for the large rooms with huge sash windows, which make their home light, bright and airy, and because there was plenty of space next door to house their company's weaving looms and design studio. But there wasn't much else to recommend the place. It had what an estate agent might call 'lots of potential' – in other words, no heating or electricity and only two bathrooms for six bedrooms; everywhere was in dire need of redecorating. It took six months to strip it bare, rewire it and install central heating, and another six to add three new bathrooms and make it properly habitable.

Sticking to their goal of combining comfort, flexibility and simplicity, the couple instinctively gravitated towards a neutral background palette when it came to decoration. They were fortunate still to have original floorboards in the sitting room and hall, which they sanded and stained darker; elsewhere they laid sisal carpeting, covered with their own felt or linen

'WE HATE PRETENTIOUSNESS IN INTERIORS. WE ALWAYS WANT TO HAVE ONLY THE THINGS WE LIKE AROUND US AND TO USE THEM. IT'S A QUESTION OF GETTING YOUR PRIORITIES RIGHT.'

LEFT **Roger and Fay visit a great number of trade fairs as part of their work; they bought this sweet bent-chestnut tub chair and table in France.**

ABOVE AND OPPOSITE **Calm colours predominate in the snug, while deep reds add warmth and vitality. The feel is casual; the large cushion cover** on the sofa, for example, was once a grain sack. Although the couple never consciously buy antiques, they found the old armoire at a local dealer.

THE SPARE FORMS AND PLAIN COLOURS THAT MAKE UP THE INTERIOR ARE NOT ONLY SIMPLE BUT ALSO VERY SOPHISTICATED, TENDING TOWARDS AN ALMOST URBAN, MINIMAL ETHOS, ALBEIT ONE TEMPERED BY INTERESTING TEXTURES AND AN OVERALL FEELING OF RELAXATION.

ABOVE LEFT **The centrepiece of one of the new bathrooms is a lovely old rolltop bath. The large drying rack rigged up around the shower functions perfectly as a screen.**

ABOVE RIGHT **Roger and Fay painted the floorboards of the bathroom, and added one of their signature striped runners.**

RIGHT **Convenient storage for bathroom bits and pieces.**

OPPOSITE **Piled on the travel chest at the foot of the bed are blankets from an occasional range designed by Fay and produced by Roger. The waffle-weave bedspread is Austrian.**

rugs in understated designs. In the sitting room and the snug ('the room we use all the time'), they introduced a dash of warmth and interest in the form of vibrant crimson on some of the walls and upholstery. Curtains, cushions and throws tend also towards utter simplicity, in the form of chocolate or natural linens and wools from the Roger Oates collection, while the furniture is a combination of old and new things that they have simply found and liked, from 'twig' chairs and tables to baskets and antique chests.

'We haven't particularly inherited any furniture, and we would never consciously aim to buy an antique. We have just gone out, seen things and bought them,' says Roger. 'At the end of the day, Fay and I wanted to be modern and we wanted to be comfortable. And we've shown that the two can go together.'

designer retreat

Imagine having a fashion designer look you up and down, consider your proportions and then decide how best to dress you in order to stress your good points and disguise your worst. Such was the fate of this mill house in Oxfordshire, which had a complete makeover by couturier Bruce Oldfield. Oldfield transformed the mill from a dowdy bed-and-breakfast into a gloriously stylish country retreat.

Bruce Oldfield has a talent for interior design, and a proven ability to translate his eye for colour and proportion from clothing bodies to dressing rooms. He has always taken a close interest in the look of his shops and has plans to expand into interior design, perhaps beginning with a small range of furniture.

When he discovered the mill (now his former home), it was the setting of water meadows and fields that attracted him, rather than the building itself. The Georgian brickwork had been punctuated with replacement diamond-pane windows and the interior had been divided into a warren of rooms. 'It wasn't so much a domestic building as an industrial building – more like a loft or a warehouse in a field,' says Oldfield. Opening out became the decorative theme of the whole house, which now has many fewer bedrooms but a spectacular sense of space. The main living room, which has a door leading through to the

ABOVE The central living room is double height with a wide galleried landing running around two sides. The walls in this room were originally bare brick in a dark, rusty red, and the beams were dark brown. The result was a gloomy, ersatz rusticity, which was banished by painting bricks and beams a soft off-white.

RIGHT Oldfield added to the drama of this lofty space with substantial pieces such as the enormous pots on the table behind the sofa.

LEFT The sense of openness in the old mill was enhanced by the furnishings, which were few but large, such as this plump chaise longue.

ABOVE **Oldfield's pottery and old bone-handled knives fitted perfectly with the rustic sophistication of the kitchen.**

RIGHT **In the kitchen, everyday items were laid out for all to see, while glasses were stored in a transparent cabinet. The spaces beneath the kitchen units and the predominance of open shelving maximized the view of the new slate floor and expanded the sense of space.**

OPPOSITE, ABOVE **The original stable-style back door opens straight into the kitchen.**

OPPOSITE, BELOW **Pieces such as this beautifully turned antique chair added the charm of the genuinely hand-made.**

garden and a French window giving onto a balcony over the millrace, is double height up to the beamed roof. This gives the room the exhilarating volume of a church or an ancient barn. A simple gallery of white-painted banisters runs around two sides of the room, allowing space for an open-plan library, a tempting place to sit and read while surveying the view below.

The room is so big that Oldfield divided it into zones. Helping to mark these out were two large, bound-sisal mats laid over the floorboards. One of these was stretched in front of the fireplace, where a sofa and armchairs invited relaxation. The other covered the second half of the room, where there was a dining table next to the stairs leading down to the kitchen.

The sense of openness was enhanced by the furnishings, which were large and few. A huge sketch of Oldfield's Rhodesian Ridgeback hung over the fireplace. Propped to its right was a tall mirror, which reflected the windows in a long enfilade of light. A pair of giant china pots held small trees on the table behind the sofa, and even the cushions were extra large. Walls and woodwork were white and off-white, making the most of the abundant daylight.

RIGHT **The bathroom is large, if awkwardly shaped, allowing enough space for those ultimate bathroom luxuries, a sofa and a wardrobe.**

OPPOSITE, FAR RIGHT, ABOVE AND BELOW **Tucked into the steep pitch of the roof, the bathroom, like the bedroom, is reminiscent of a barn. The sloping ceiling adds character but is far from practical.**

OLDFIELD'S INSTINCT WAS TO OPEN OUT THE HOUSE AND MAKE THE MOST OF THE LOVELY SETTING BY GIVING AS MANY ROOMS AS POSSIBLE DIRECT ACCESS TO THE OUTSIDE.

By knocking out more walls, Oldfield made a kitchen, which fills the whole ground floor with windows on every side. Instead of opting for a rustic look, he chose a freestanding, modular kitchen. 'I liked the clash of its slightly industrial, modern looks with the country feel of the beams and windows,' he says.

At the top of the house the main bedroom and bathroom were squeezed into the triangle of the roof – a potentially uncomfortable arrangement for a man of Oldfield's stature. Bath and bed had to be placed away from the walls, to give enough ceiling height. The bath was freestanding, and the bed was anchored in the middle of the room by a set of shelves that doubled as clothes storage and bedhead.

ABOVE **Black and white photographs of Oldfield and his two foster brothers, taken in 1957, were blown up and hung on the bedroom wall in matching wooden frames, making them look more like artworks than family snaps.**

RIGHT **The only comfortable place for a bed in a room of this shape is in the middle. The chunky set of open shelves served the dual purpose of providing a solid and protective bedhead and taking the place of a bedside table.**

picture credits

Key: ph=photographer, a=above, b=below, r=right, l=left, c=centre.

Endpapers ph Jan Baldwin/Roderick & Gillie James' house in Devon designed by Roderick James Architects and built by Carpenter Oak Ltd; page 1 ph Chris Tubbs/Phil Lapworth's treehouse near Bath; **2–5** ph Chris Tubbs; **6–7** ph Simon Upton/the Jacomini Family Farm, designed by Jacomini Interior Design; **8–9** ph Simon Upton/The Crooked House; **10–11** & **12al** ph Simon Upton/the home of Julia and Glen Vague, Kentucky, designed by Jacomini Interior Design; **12bl** ph Simon Upton/the Jacomini Family Farm, designed by Jacomini Interior Design; **12br** ph Simon Upton/Conner Prairie, an open-air living-history museum located in central Indiana; **12–13a** ph Christopher Drake/Florence and Pierre Pallardy, Domaine de la Baronnie, St-Martin de Ré; **13bl** ph Simon Upton/Mrs Robin Elverson's house near Round Top, Texas; **13ar** ph Simon Upton/Conner Prairie, an open-air living-history museum located in central Indiana; **14–19** ph Simon Upton/Conner Prairie, an open-air living-history museum located in central Indiana; **20–25** ph Simon Upton/the home of Julia and Glen Vague, Kentucky, designed by Jacomini Interior Design; **26–31** ph Christopher Drake/Florence and Pierre Pallardy, Domaine de la Baronnie, St-Martin de Ré; **32–37** ph Simon Upton/the Jacomini Family Farm, designed by Jacomini Interior Design; **38–43** ph Simon Upton/a residence in Highlands, North Carolina, designed by Nancy Braithwaite Interiors; **44–53** ph Alan Williams/Louise Robbins' house in North West Herefordshire; **54–59** ph Christopher Drake/A country house near Mougins, Provence; **60–65** Simon Upton/Interior Designer JoAnn R. Barwick's house in Connecticut; **66–73** ph Alan Williams/The Norfolk home of Geoff & Gilly Newberry of Bennison Fabrics. All fabrics by Bennison cabinet-maker, Victor Clark; **74–75** ph Simon Upton; **76al** & **76bl** ph Simon Upton/The Crooked House; **76ar** & **77al** ph Chris Tubbs/Daniel Jasiak's home near Biarritz; **76br–77bl** & **77br** ph Jan Baldwin/Roderick & Gillie James' house in Devon designed by Roderick James Architects and built by Carpenter Oak Ltd; **78–83** ph Simon Upton/The Crooked House; **84–89** ph Simon Upton/Mrs Robin Elverson's house near Round Top, Texas; **90–95** ph Simon Upton/A Chalet in Verbier designed by Todhunter Earle Interiors; **96–101** ph Jan Baldwin/Roderick & Gillie James' house in Devon designed by Roderick James Architects and built by Carpenter Oak Ltd; **102–107** ph Chris Tubbs/Daniel Jasiak's home near Biarritz; **108–13** ph Ray Main/Marina & Peter Hill's barn in West Sussex designed by Marina Hill, Peter James Construction Management, Chichester, The West Sussex Antique Timber Company, Wisborough Green, and Joanna Jefferson Architects; **114–19** ph Christopher Drake/Diana Bauer's house near Cotignac, styling by Enrica Stabile; **120–21** ph Lina Ikse Bergman/Ceramicist Jette Arendal Winther & Composer Niels Winther's home in Denmark; **122al** ph Christopher Drake/Melanie Thornton's former home in Gloucestershire.; **122bl** ph Christopher Drake/Annie-Camille Kuentzmann-Levet's house in the Yvelines; **122br** ph Christopher Drake/Ali Sharland's former home in Gloucestershire; **122–23a** ph Simon Upton/Lena Proudlock's home Gloucestershire that has since been restyled; **123r** ph Christopher Drake/A country house in the Lubéron, with interior design by François Gilles and Dominque Lubar of IPL Interiors and Pierre-Marie Gilles – Paris; **123bl** ph Alan Williams/The Arbuthnott family's house near Cirencester designed by Nicholas Arbuthnott, interior design & fabrics by Vanessa Arbuthnott; **124–31** ph Lina Ikse Bergman/Ceramicist Jette Arendal Winther & Composer Niels Winther's home in Denmark; **132–35** ph Christopher Drake/Melanie Thornton's former home in Gloucestershire; **136–41** Simon Upton/Lena Proudlock's home in Gloucestershire that has since been restyled; **142–45** ph Alan Williams/The Arbuthnott family's house near Cirencester designed by Nicholas Arbuthnott, interior design & fabrics by Vanessa Arbuthnott; **146–151** ph Christopher Drake/Annie-Camille Kuentzmann-Levet's house in the Yvelines; **152–57** ph Christopher Drake/Ali Sharland's former home in Gloucestershire; **158–63** ph Christopher Drake/A country house in the Lubéron, with interior design by François Gilles and Dominque Lubar of IPL Interiors and Pierre-Marie Gilles – Paris; **164–169** ph Christopher Drake/Monique Davidson's family home in Normandy; **170–71** ph Simon Upton; **172al** & **172bl** ph Simon Upton/A cottage in Oxfordshire designed by Ann Boyd; **172ar–73al** & **173bl** ph Andrew Wood/Fay & Roger Oates' house in Ledbury; **172br** & **173ar** ph Christopher Drake/Eva Johnson's house in Suffolk, interiors designed by Eva Johnson; **174–79** ph Simon Upton/A cottage in Oxfordshire designed by Ann Boyd; **180–85** ph Simon Upton; **186–91** ph Jan Baldwin/Mark Smith's home in the Cotswolds; **192–97** ph Jan Baldwin/The owner of Tessuti, Catherine Vindevogel–Debal's house in Kortrijk, Belgium. Kitchen designed by Filip Van Bever; **198–201** ph Christopher Drake/Eva Johnson's house in Suffolk, interiors designed by Eva Johnson; **202–207** ph Debi Treloar/Kristiina Ratia and Jeff Gocke's family home in Norwalk, Connecticut; **208–13** ph Andrew Wood/Fay & Roger Oates' house in Ledbury; **214–19** ph Christopher Drake/Bruce Oldfield's former home in Oxfordshire.

architects and designers whose work is featured in this book

Ali Sharland

Sharland & Lewis

52 Long Street

Tetbury

Gloucestershire GL8 8AQ

01666 500354

www.sharlandandlewis.com

Pages 122br, 152–57.

Ann Boyd Design Ltd

33 Elystan Street

London SW3 3NT

020 7591 0202

Pages 172al, 172bl, 174–79.

Annie-Camille Kuentzmann-Levet

Décoration

3 Ter, rue Mathieu Le Coz

La Noue

78980 Mondreville

France

+ 33 1 30 42 53 59

Pages 122bl, 146–51.

Bennison

16 Holbein Place

London SW1W 8NL

020 7730 8076

bennisonfabrics@btinternet.com

www.bennisonfabrics.com

Pages 66–73.

Bruce Oldfield Ltd

27 Beauchamp Place

London SW31NJ

020 7584 1363

info@bruceoldfield.com

Pages 214–19.

Carpenter Oak Ltd

The Framing Yard

East Cornworthy

Totnes

Devon TQ9 7HF

01803 732 900

www.carpenteroak.com

Pages 76br–77bl, 77br, 96–101, endpapers.

Collection Privée Antiquités

Isabelle Schouten

www.collection-privee.com

Pages 54–59.

Conner Prairie

13400 Allisonville Road

Fishers, IN 46038

USA

+ 1 800 966 1836

www.connerprairie.org

Open-air living-history museum.

Pages 12br, 13ar, 14–19.

Daniel Jasiak

Designer

12 rue Jean Ferrandi

Paris 75006

France

+ 33 01 45 49 13 56

Pages 76ar, 77al, 102–107.

Domaine de la Baronnie

21 rue Baron de Chantal

17410 St-Martin de Ré

France

+ 33 5 46 09 21 29

info@labaronnie-pallardy.com

www.labaronnie-pallardy.com

Pages 12–13a, 26–31.

Enrica Stabile

L'Utile e il Dilettevole

via della Spiga 46

Milan

Italy

+ 39 02 76 00 84 20

www.enricastabile.com

Antiques dealer, interior decorator

and photographic stylist.

Pages 114–19.

Eva Johnson

Interior Designer

01638 731 362

www.evajohnson.com

Distributor of TRIP TRAP products

for the treatment of wooden floors.

Pages 172br, 173ar, 198–201.

Filip Van Bever

Filipvanbever@skynet.be

Kitchen design.

Pages 192–97.

IPL Interiors

25 Bullen Street

Battersea

London SW11 3ER

020 7978 4224

Pages 123r, 158–63.

J&M Davidson

gallery

97 Golborne Road

London W10 5NL

shop

42 Ledbury Road

London W11 2SE

Pages 164–69.

Jacomini Interior Design
1701 Brun Street, Suite 101
Houston, TX 77019
USA
+ 1 713 524 8224
www.jacominidesign.com
Pages 6–7, 10–11, 12al, 12bl, 20–25, 32–37.

Jette Arendal Winther
Arendal Keramisk Vaerksted
Tvaervej 10
3390 Hundested
Denmark
+ 45 47 98 27 63
www.arendal-ceramics.com
Pages 120–21, 124–31.

JoAnn Barwick Interiors
PO Box 982
Boca Grande, FL 33921
USA
Pages 60–65.

Joanna Jefferson Architects
222 Oving Road
Chichester
West Sussex PO19 4EJ
01243 532 398
jjeffearch@aol.com
Pages 108–13.

Kristiina Ratia Designs
+ 1 203 852 0027
Pages 202–207.

Lena Proudlock/Denim in Style
01666 500051
www.deniminstyle.co.uk
Pages 122ar–23al, 136–41.

Louise Robbins
Insideout House and Garden Agency and
Malt House Bed & Breakfast
Almeley
Herefordshire HR3 6PY
01544 340681
lulawrence1@aol.com
www.insideout-house&garden.co.uk
Pages 44–53.

Mark Smith at Smithcreative
15 St Georges Road
London W4 1AU
020 8747 3909
mark@smithcreative.net
Ceramics by David Garland,
01285 720307.
Pages 186–91.

Melanie Thornton/Feels Like Home
Home style consultant
07802 286068
Pages 122al, 132–35.

Nancy Braithwaite Interiors
2300 Peachtree Road, Suite C101
Atlanta, GA 30309
USA
+ 1 404 355 1740
Pages 38–43.

Roderick James Architects
Seagull House
Dittisham Mill Creek
Dartmouth
Devon TQ6 0HZ
01803 722474
www.roderickjamesarchitects.com
An architectural practice specializing in
contemporary wood and glass buildings.
Pages 76br–77bl, 77br, 96–101, endpapers.

Roger Oates
London showroom
1 Munro Terrace (off Riley Street)
London SW10 0DL
020 7351 2288

Eastnor shop
The Long Barn
Eastnor
Herefordshire HR8 1EL
01531 631611
www.rogeroates.co.uk
Pages 172–73a & 173bl, 208–13.

Simon Kimmins Design and
Project Control
020 8314 1526
Page 1.

Tessuti
Interiors & Fabrics
Doorniksewijk 76
8500 Kortrijk
Belgium
+ 32 56 25 29 27
info@tessuti.be
www.tessuti.be
Pages 192–97.

Tia Swan
The Crooked House
Bed & Breakfast
PO Box 13
Knighton
Powys LD8 2WE
Pages 8–9, 76al, 76bl, 78–83.

Todhunter Earle
Chelsea Reach, 1st Floor
79–89 Lots Road
London SW10 0RN
020 7349 9999
www.todhunterearle.com
enquiries@todhunterearle.com
Pages 90–95.

Vanessa Arbuthnott
fabrics
www.vanessaarbuthnott.co.uk
holiday lets
www.thetallet.co.uk
Pages 123bl, 142–45.

index

Italics indicate picture captions.